Empty Shoes

Poems on the Hungry
and the Homeless

Selected and Edited
by
Patrick T. Randolph

D1279922

Popcorn Press
P.O. Box 12
Elkhorn, WI 53121

Cover Design: Katheryn Smith
Photo Credits: Haluk Asna,
                Gamze & Patrick T. Randolph,
                & Katrin Talbot
Typesetting: Lester Smith

This anthology is for my wife, Gamze,
my soul's *real* home,
and to each and every homeless
and hungry person,
may these pages help you in some small way.

A special thanks of warmth and cheer to
my precious American and Turkish families,
Popcorn Press, members of the LAWG,
the poets of this project,
and to my friends around the globe.

Table of Contents

Part I

Part II

Part III

Part IV

Part V

Special Gratitude

This volume of poems would not be complete without a special heartfelt note of appreciation to my wife, Gamze. The hours she spent typing the manuscript while I edited the poems was a dance of the most beautiful kind. Her support for the project from the moment it was conceived to the final stages of editing was a continual breath of life-soul-grin inspiring air. I could not have done this without her. I thank her for being here.

In Memoriam

John Wyatt (1937-2008) and Ayfer Asna (1952-2008) have kept countless bodies and souls from becoming homeless—both spiritually and physically. John was my mentor at Beloit College, teaching me everything from Pre-Socratic Philosophy to how to be a true human being. John's love for teaching took him and his wife to work with terminally ill patients in California. His love for learning inspired him to work with minority children in Beloit. Ayfer was my beloved mother-in-law who passed away in October of 2008 due to cancer. She taught English in the public and private schools in Istanbul, Turkey, for 26 years. Her influence on students and their lives has been incredible. Both John and Ayfer were dedicated teachers and learners of life; they were believers in the goodness of the human soul and sincere poets of the human spirit. They have influenced me, my wife, and others in countless ways. Their corporeal presence will be greatly missed, but their spiritual echoes will continue to bless this great grinning green earth and all its wonders.

Acknowledgements

The editor and poets of this anthology would like to warmly thank the following publications in which these poems first appeared, some in slightly different versions.

A Place to Keep Time Spent (Poetry Collection): "O" & "We Must Away"

Big Scream: "William"

Blind Man's Rainbow: "Precarious"

Ceremony Collected Anthology: "Michigan Avenue"

Ceremony: A Journal of Poetry and Other Arts: "Origin of Homelessness"

Christian Citizen: "Feet on the Subway" (Also published in *Backstreet Quarterly*)

Clark Street Review: "Anna"

Curiosity to Satisfy and Fear to Placate (Poetry Collection): "Our Dissolving Histories"

Free Verse: "Apéritif," "Brain Food," & "Mother and Child"

Geronimo Review: "Small Change"

Goose River Anthology 2007: "Under a St. Louis Bridge"

Goose River Anthology 2008: "Empty Shoes"

HazMat: A Literary Review: "Poverty Grants the Exclusive"

Illogical Muse: "Hungry Cats"

Irish Stew: "Homeless Minstrel," "Istanbul at Dawn," & "Empty Shoes"

Istanbul Literary Review: "The Truth about Cats and Dogs"

Kupozine: "Elder Park"

Leaven Works!: "At the Intake Desk"

Long Island Quarterly: "Into the Light: Safe Haven 1944" (Also published in *Voices Israel 2007* & *Poetica*)

Papyrus: "Eighteenth Birthday"

Pawpars: "Ides of March"

Poetry Depth Quarterly: "Chicago's Grant Park"

Something Near the Dance Floor (Poetry Collection): "White Stallions"

Street Views (Homeless Newspaper: Wyoming): "Cardboard Box"

The Orange Room Review: "Shopping List"

The Rockford River Times: "Human Economics"

The Rockford Review: "Winter Classroom"

The Seventh Quarry: "Stranger"

Thunder Lake (Poetry Collection): "Late October Evening"

Tonguebones (Poetry Collection): "Feed Them"

Tsigan: The Gypsy Poem: A selected poem appears from this collection.

Umbrella: "What They Dream About at the Shelter"

Write On!: "Alley Row"

Awards

Wilda Morris' "Feet on the Subway" received a third-place honor for the *Evanston Public Library Poetry Contest* in 2000. Patrick T. Randolph's "Winter Classroom" received second-place honors for *The Rockford Review*'s *2008 Ides of March Poetry Contest*. Mary Jo Balistreri's "Lady of the Rising Steam," David S. Pointer's "hubcap dinner plates," and Jenna Rindo's "Homeless but Known on a First-Name Basis" were winning poems for the 2008 *Free Verse Magazine Poetry Contest on the Homeless*.

Photo Credits & Information

Haluk Asna: Untitled, Izmir, Turkey, page 227.

Gamze Randolph: "City Lights Bookstore," San Francisco, CA, page xvi; "Empty Shoes," Istanbul, Turkey, pages 1 & 212; "Collected Stories," Murdo, SD, page 32; "Home in the Wind," San Francisco, CA, page 70; "Fire-Soaked Forest," Yellowstone National Park, page 174.

Patrick T. Randolph: "After First Light," La Crosse, WI, page 17; "Small Change," San Francisco, CA, page 25; "Taking Flight," San Francisco, CA, page 40; "Winter Sunset," Tuzla, Istanbul, Turkey, page 43; "Evening Rounds," San Francisco, CA, page 59; "Through the Pines," Gooseberry Falls State Park, MN, page 72; "Late Summer Falls," Gooseberry Falls State Park, MN, page 74; "Open Eyes," San Francisco, CA, page

83; "Forest Voices," Gooseberry Falls State Park, MN, page 86; "Last-Chance Motel," page 108; "Shopping Cart Village," San Francisco, CA, page 114; "Early Spring Snow," La Crosse, WI, page 118; "Finding the Way," La Crosse, WI, page 137; "Endless Vision," Alcatraz, San Francisco, CA, page 140; "Pondering the Sun," Albany, CA, page 156; "Where Angels Walk," Istanbul, Turkey, page 164; "Snow Songs at Noon," Istanbul, Turkey, page 188; "Lamplight," Alcatraz, San Francisco, CA, page 206; "Where They Once Sat," San Francisco, CA, page 209.

Katrin Talbot: "Hard Times," Portland, OR, page 97; "Keeping Watch," Honolulu, HI, page 110; "House Keeping," Honolulu, HI, page 124; "Pane," Janesville, WI, page 159; "To Have, to Give, to Receive," Cape Cod, MA, page 168; "Embrace," Portland, OR, page 184.

City Lights Bookstore

Introductory Note on *Empty Shoes*

Jean-Jacques Rousseau wisely claimed that "The essential thing is to be good to the people with whom one lives." [1] This is echoed in Jack Kerouac's *The Scripture of the Golden Eternity*, "Kindness and sympathy, understanding and encouragement, these give: they are better than just presents and gifts: no reason in the world why not. Anyhow, be nice."[2] The motive of wanting to be good, wanting to be kind, is the fundamental force behind this poetry project for the hungry and the homeless.

I have worked directly with the hungry and the homeless in both Chicago and San Francisco. I seem to bump into them—or seek them out—wherever my wife and I go, in the States or abroad. My work with them and our chance meetings have made one truth very clear: *They* do not always fit into the easily constructed categories of being lazy freeloaders and insane drug addicts as they are often portrayed in American films, but rather, each homeless or hungry individual that I have worked with or met in passing has had a unique story that defines his or her special existence.

Empty Shoes: Poems on the Hungry and the Homeless is the result of three desires eagerly intertwined: the aspiration to raise awareness of

---

[1] Jean-Jacques Rousseau, *Emile or On Education*, trans. Alan Bloom (US: Basic Books, 1979) 30.

[2] Jack Kerouac, *The Scripture of the Golden Eternity* (New York: Corinth Book, 1960) 53.

the homeless and the hungry, the yearning to bring together insightful poetry written by kindhearted souls, and the desire to make a difference for a homeless or a hungry person.

The poets in this volume come from many backgrounds: counselors for the homeless, persons who were once homeless themselves, Midwestern farmers, schoolteachers, nurses, lawyers, professors, janitors, students, sheet-metal workers, and bartenders. The verse collected in this volume will make your spirit soar and sink with insights into the echoes of a life that is all too common on the streets of our modern civilization.

Profits from this anthology will go to benefit homeless shelters and food shelters alike throughout the country. We hope to make a humble contribution to as many individuals and shelters as we can through our poetry and through our desire to assist those who are struggling to create a decent life. Please enjoy this offering from poets who truly care, from poets who are striving to make a sincere and responsible difference in the lives of their fellow human beings.

Patrick T. Randolph

❧ I ☙

Rejoice always,
Pray without ceasing,
In everything give thanks…

                          1 Thessalonians 5:16-18

Empty Shoes

Empty Shoes

Old shoes—rain soaked street—
Pair of lonesome leather soles:
Used, worn, forgotten.

Enlightened eyes grab these gems—
Homeless man gives them a home!

Patrick T. Randolph
La Crosse, Wisconsin

Lady of the Rising Steam

Philadelphia, November 1976

Into the ice-edged darkness, my husband
and I hurried in the weak light of jaundiced
lanterns, design of old Ben Franklin.
Chestnut vendors huddled into themselves,
their fiery coals hissing and sparking.
The wind howled as we came around the
corner on Walnut Street, ripped off my hand-
loomed scarf and sent it flying behind me.
I didn't know it was gone until I heard the voice,
a wailing cry in the night. Turning, I saw
the woman crouched over the grate, red silk
scarf wildly thrashing from a withered hand.
She was unkempt, her face pocked and ridged
with wrinkles. Garments of neglect hung
on the skeletal frame as she hovered in the warmth
of the manhole's rising steam. We stopped,
uncertain. She grabbed the hem of my coat.
Fear met the madness of her roving eye.

In the shelter of our car, she spoke in the cultivated
language of art and architecture, insisted that
her son was a great commercial artist.
We talked close to an hour before we scrunched
some bills into her hand, gave her our address
and drove away. She bent back into the black
starless night and we reentered our comfortable life.

Months later, we were stunned when a police captain
called to tell us she was dead, our name in her pocket,
the only clue to her life. A life we had forgotten.
I began to mourn this lady of the rising steam,

3

replaying that night, pondering the disconnect
in her, in us.

Thirty years later, she is still the face I don't know,
and the face I'd know anywhere. She was the Sphinx
at the crossroads, and though I failed the questions,
they changed my life. Sometimes on foggy nights,
or walking the cracked sidewalks of my small town,
I see the open hand so near, the bent body I want
to call back.

Mary Jo Balistreri
Waukesha, Wisconsin

Homeless but Known on a First-Name Basis

*The foxes have holes, and the birds of the air have nests;
but the Son of man has no place to lay his head.*
Mathew 8:20

Riding home from my shift
as a nursing assistant on the neuro floor—
metal fenders on my retro Ross
keeping my whites mud-free—
I'd glide to a stop and chat up Victor.

He usually paced the right side of Grace Street,
or perhaps it was the wrong side
depending on perspective.
We exchanged our certain smells—
me stinking of Ensure[3] tube feedings,
pseudomonas, baby powder to ease the
application of a thigh-high compression hose—
Victor—harboring the heavy notes
or pipe smoke and nervous perspiration.

He'd occasionally send me on an errand,
pressing his crumpled money firmly into my
contaminated palm.
I'd chant his list aloud
like a benediction
as I pedaled off toward the Seven Eleven:
sardines, tobacco,

Townhouse crackers,
pineapple tidbits…

---

[3] *Ensure* is a medical supplement for patients who do
not eat enough to sustain their health.

5

Empty Shoes

I never thought to ask
if he had a can opener.

Jenna Rindo
Pickett, Wisconsin

hubcap dinner plates
hold bountiful stew
in the hobo camp

David S. Pointer
Murfreesboro, Tennessee

Self

No self is left—
    no one here,
    no one home.

The house is empty,
    unshuttered.

The breeze blows through—
    clean house,
    clean heart,
    good self,

Home.

P.C. Moorehead
North Lake, Wisconsin

Homeless in the City

"Hey, there, buddy! Careful
stepping over my body while
I'm trying to sleep on this pavement
that the city owns. No, the cold
don't bother me at all. See, I got
a couple layers of sweaters
wrapped up pretty good in this old
army blanket I got from
World War II. I can stand the cold,
been sleeping here for years.
No, I don't want to go to a shelter.
Can't stand the snoring.
Thanks for the hot coffee, though.
But why did you put sugar in it?
I take mine plain."

Ed Galing
Hatboro, Pennsylvania

Saint Ben's

Five p.m. on Milwaukee's State Street,
driving west out of downtown—
traffic slows,
dusk settles.

Hunger's long line curves
down the steps
and fills the sidewalk
for the block around
St. Benedict's Catholic Church.

The wait
for a warm meal:
    men,
    women,
    a few children.

They wait
on this cold rainy November night,
a few have black umbrellas—
most have no protection
from the downpour.

I go home
to a warm house,
spilling with food—
no longer hungry.

Janet Leahy
New Berlin, Wisconsin

Dear Sir

I am sorry about the tourist
in the printed shirt
who took your picture Sunday
as you slept on the sidewalk
in Key West.

It came as a surprise to me
to see him focus his camera on you
while his family snickered
and watched.

I found his actions
offensive—

Please, accept my apology.

Janet Leahy
New Berlin, Wisconsin

A House Off the Beaten Path

I've often thought
to ring its bell
on the door that shuts
only to trap the warmth

inside. Pane after pane
a glow, the hearth ablaze;
Over and over
I reach for the bell.

Ruth Sabath Rosenthal
New York City, New York

I Don't Know His Name

I don't know his name, but I'll forever remember
his full-throttled rendition of *Amazing Grace* at a
    New York
subway stop on 53rd Street. People hurried past him,
past his outstretched hand with its tightly gripped
paper cup. Even though it was summer, he wore
multi-layered pants, three shirts, a jacket, a long
    black coat,
and a battered backpack held together with safety pins.
His head tossed back, voice aimed upward, lifting
    to be heard
above the screeching brakes of the trains. I didn't
    fight
the wave of humanity trying to board the subway.
I cannot remember what the air felt like that day,
    whether
it was grief or a splinter of fear that knuckled my
    heart, but
I lost something by not being able to drop money
    into his cup.
The hunger, his voice, *Amazing Grace*—the
    memory of it washing
over me, the frail bridge on which we traveled
    toward
each other—that one moment that broke us apart.

Ellen Kort
Appleton, Wisconsin

13

Feeding the Pigeons

From his sack he draws golden
bread crumbs, scatters them at his feet.
As if by invisible signal they come—
the hungry and the opportune.

Their feathers catch the sun setting
over his bent shoulders. Dressed
in tuxedos of quick-silver gray,
mottled white-brown, iridescent
blue-black, they feed on his fine fare.

Sack empty, he walks back
to his alcove in the stone wall,
lies down on his bed of paper and rags—

St. Francis of Budapest closes his eyes and sleeps.

Susan F. Kirch-Thibado
Menomonie, Wisconsin

Standing

I open the door,
and the many poor, they stand,
    hearts opened,
    hands stretched out,
    emptied by life—
The many poor,
    they stand.

The rich deprived,
    the deprived rich,
    the wealthy poor,
    the poor wealthy—
Hands outstretched,
    they stand.

P.C. Moorehead
North Lake, Wisconsin

Old Man on Bench

You sit staring
at your shoes—
unable to see beyond
the brown of your next step.

Susan F. Kirch-Thibado
Menomonie, Wisconsin

After First Light

Seasons

I seeded my shoes for the journey
    from a packet unnamed.
Deep in the earth, I seeded them,
    moist from the winter rains.
Working, I tilled them,
    raking the leaves away.

I seeded my shoes for the journey,
    not knowing the ending way,
Hoping the sun would reach them,
    warming their roots each day.
I seeded my shoes for the journey—
    and in spring the flowers came.

P.C. Moorehead
North Lake, Wisconsin

Stopping

I am lost in the rain.
It washes over me,
    cleansing me,
    burying me in its torrent,
    carrying away the color of myself.

My skin pales,
    My eyes fade;
I stand there,
    inviting invisibility.

The rain stops.
    My skin darkens,
    My eyes brighten,
    My hair shimmers.

Someone stops and looks.
"Why, you're so pretty,
    you could stop traffic."
I stand there,
    visible.

P.C. Moorehead
North Lake, Wisconsin

Too Young to Be Old

I am possessed by an angry humor,
A cankered soul cut with woe and rage,
I sit alone like an old man
And count my cigarettes 'til noon—
Forced to contemplate the stares of strangers.

This day is awash in gray,
Dark sidewalks, cold cement—
Sloppy wet newspapers.

My spirit I hold tight
Through vague, sluggish perception—

I've died many times, yet I wake each day to live.

Dave Dolle
La Crosse, Wisconsin

Chicago's Grant Park

Homeless woman's hands:
Old, dirty, cuts everywhere—
Lifeless, cold fingers;

In this morning's harsh sunlight
They hold seeds and wait—for birds.

Patrick T. Randolph
La Crosse, Wisconsin

Bitter Roots

I never sold apples
during the Depression

on that New York
street that I passed by each day.

You would find them,
men with wooden crates upon

which the apples rested, and below
the sign hung:
>   "BUY AN APPLE AND HELP
>   ME—5 CENTS."

The men always looked so sad
and old before their time;

millions unemployed—
and I too was one of them,

existing on a welfare check
once a month.

Often I would shiver in
the cold air; I'd stop and buy
an apple on the way
to nothing,

thinking it could be me,
it could be me;

and from then on
an apple never tasted
the same again.

Ed Galing
Hatboro, Pennsylvania

Feet on the Subway

His coat was ragged
as his face. His worn hat
and threadbare gloves
could not protect him
from the icy cold racing
through the wind tunnels
of New York City.
Probably he panhandled
coins to ride the subway.
My eyes were drawn
from his sunken face,
his recessed eyes,
to the skin of his ankles
stretched tight and red,
his puffy feet, pressed
into loafers, the newspaper
stuffing visible through
large holes in the soles.
I shivered less from the cold
than the coldness
with which I stared.
I reached my station
and left the subway,
but took his feet with me.
Look, the swollen ankles,
the newspaper-stuffed shoes
are still stored
just behind
my eyes.

Wilda Morris
Bolingbrook, Illinois

Small Change

Contingencies

In Azcapotzalco,
I remember mostly
their dark eyes,
their round, brown faces,
Mexican bowl haircuts,
and then,
the outstretched, dirty palms
with ragged fingernails,
those tiny hands
on the end of spindly arms.

In Weligama,
they encircled us.
Their dry, cracked lips begging
for a twopence.
"One two piece, one two piece,"
They chanted.
Clad, mummy-like in rags,
gray from the mud of streets.
The filth of poverty—
Their smiles engaging.

I have seen them in Cairo,
near the City of the Dead,
where the deceased "live" better
than the living.
Hauntingly beautiful children,
maimed, crippled, scarred
by their parents
in order to elicit pity,
hence the silver and copper coins
from rich American tourists.

In Lima, in front of the Cathedral
which held the catafalques
and Pizarro's tomb,
a gypsy woman tried to hand me
a baby, pleading,
"Un regalo, un regalo."
As I reached out for her "gift,"
You held me back.
"Don't take it," you hissed.
"She'll run away."
I stood there,
in the shadow
of the basilica—
in somber half-light,
in the cobbled streets
of this foreign city—
my barren heart,
my fallow womb
needing the baby,

But you pulled me away.

Sharmagne Leland-St. John
Hollywood Hills, California

The Truth About
Cats and Dogs

He is hungry, she is homeless.
He is a dog, she is a cat.
They are really both human,
Playing games like this to keep
Each other alive.

He died last night, she'll die tomorrow—
These are not imaginative stories,
But songs of the shadows

That walk these streets day in and day out—
Call them dogs and cats if you like,
But human they are—
Hungry and homeless.

Patrick T. Randolph
La Crosse, Wisconsin

Hungry Cats

Lamp glow on the streets,
Thick mist and the sound of cats
Scampering about

In the alleyway—chasing
The shadows of mice long dead.

Patrick T. Randolph
La Crosse, Wisconsin

White Stallions

Quetzaltenango, Guatemala, 1998

The children of the street
must see themselves
in the greasy puddles of the forenoon,
in the sundown storefront windows,
in the luster of the shoes they shine;

must see themselves
in the reflection of a customer's sunglasses,
in the tears of the old women,
in the shadow of the bus.

The children of the street
must see themselves
flying purple kites on sunny beaches,
dining with the family after church,
riding white stallions—

The children of the street
must see themselves.

Bruce Dethlefsen
Westfield, Wisconsin

Feeding the Hungry

I'm not so sure a poem will feed the hungry
even as I collect canned goods at the latest benefit
    reading;
I know some people shelter their hearts with words—
building a fortress even—against the possible
    invasion of truth,
thus starving their souls of anything nourishing.

I've seen their faces in the long lines while I stand
    behind
the counter pleasantly asking, "Beans or corn?"
and quite honestly, I am skeptical that this is enough,
or maybe it's too much—the food never
seems to change the look in their eyes.

Perhaps poems are just so many words
strung together like pretty petits fours[4] when
meat and potatoes are wanting, and yet
I've heard civilizations have died for lack of poetry.

Better, perhaps, the poet as dowser, divining
    sunken streams
that flow buried and forgotten in each of us,
willowing words that strike deeply—if sometimes
    painfully—
bursting wellsprings of faith
that can truly flood a famished life.

Liz Rhodebeck
Pewaukee, Wisconsin

---

[4] *Petit four* is French meaning *small oven. Petits fours* are iced
and elaborately decorated bit-sized cakes. Traditionally they
were made from leftovers and baked while the ovens cooled
at the end of the day.

Collected Stories

Homeless Wanderer

At night I sleep in abandoned cars
That smell of loss and sweat.

I lie inside these paupers' tombs
Just one among a crowd
On a narrow, dead-end street
Where no U-turns are allowed.

I'm like the child whose tongue
Is frozen on the ice—
No one can bear to look
As he struggles to free himself.

Except, of course, for each of you
Who talk but fail to see that
You could become the wanderer
And sleep right next to me.

Susan Kileen
Watertown, Wisconsin

33

Apéritif[5]

A 100-word story

Waiting for takeout tonight, I read in the paper
that if every time you give one rat food, you give
another rat electric shocks, the first rat will stop
eating.

It made me remember a time in New York, when
I watched some police chase a homeless man away
from the front window of a sushi restaurant where
I was dining.

And how that had reminded me of suppertime as
a kid, when "The CBS Evening News with Walter
Cronkite" showed Vietnam War footage on TV.

I wonder: Could you train a rat to eat while
another one gets shocked?

Lester Smith
Delavan, Wisconsin

---

[5] An *apéritif* is a small alcoholic drink taken to stimulate
the appetite before meals.

Years Ago

Can't I lie down and die?
I wouldn't take up much space—
And, if in winter,
I wouldn't stink up the place.

It wouldn't matter too much,
Some corner to curl up in—
A patch behind the alley,
Time to harden my bones, stiffen my skin.

Can't I lie down and die,
Far away from a nursing-home bed?
Leave what's left, just pass me by—
Years ago my own ghost fled.

Dave Dolle
La Crosse, Wisconsin

Here

Here I am
    in the here
    that has no where.

Here I am
    in the where
    that is all here.

Here I am
    where I am.

    Hear!

P.C. Moorehead
North Lake, Wisconsin

Brain Food

A 100-word story

At sixteen, I worked after school at a burger joint
with an older guy whose eyes were brown as
muddy ponds.

Minimum wage was $1.60, but teenagers got $1.30.
I hated doing the same work as the mud-eyed man
for lower pay. I couldn't wait to finish school,
ditch that place, and shake its dust off my shoes
on the way out the door. What Muddy dreamed
about, I don't know.

On our breaks, he always ate fish sandwiches.
"Brain food!" he'd mumble, with one crammed in
his mouth.

I'd just nod and concentrate on homework,
cramming for tomorrow's test.

Lester Smith
Delavan, Wisconsin

Boredom

He farts his boredom away—
Open window coughs,
Another butterfly faints!

Patrick T. Randolph
La Crosse, Wisconsin

Michigan Avenue

Beggar on the street,
"Even one small cent would help,"
He sings like a song;

I pass by with a loud smile,
His eyes grin—noisy silence.

Patrick T. Randolph
La Crosse, Wisconsin

❧ **II** ☙

Observe the wonders as they occur around you.
Do not claim them. Feel the artistry
Moving through and be silent.

Rumi: "Body Intelligence II"

Taking Flight

Into the Light:
Safe Haven 1944

"And you that shall cross from shore to shore years hence
        are more to me,
and more in my meditations, than you might suppose."
                                        Walt Whitman

Thank God for you, *Henry Gibbins,*[6]
ship of dreams laden with bedraggled brethren
dark and fair, tall and short,
frail-boned and gaunt, each and every one
a survivor reborn in the wake of conscience.
Blessed, their leader, Ruth Gruber,
praised, her leader, Franklin D. Roosevelt;
and you, Captain Korn, your kind face and
        outstretched arms,
your smiling crew, their helpful hands;
your great vessel's stalwart bulk, hallowed halls
and glistening white toilets,
sky-crowned decks surrounded by sea-speckled
        rail—a far cry
from barbed wire.
Divine are you, clean fresh air that fills sunken
        chests, lungs
ashen from the fires of Auschwitz-Birkenau,
Bergen-Belsen, Buchenwald, Dachau, Treblinka.

---

[6] The *Henry Gibbins* was an army transport ship within a
naval convoy that carried the 982 "most needy" of the
holocaust survivors out of Europe, to Manhattan, NY,
en route to the refugee camp "Ft. Ontario" in Oswego,
NY, arriving August 3, 1944. The exodus named "Safe
Haven" is memorialized in a museum there.

Revered are you, buoyant sea, your strong currents
    and changing tides,
gulls that glide the breeze and assuage wounded
    spirit;
and you, dining halls bejeweled with vegetables,
    cornucopia
of meats, kaleidoscope of sweets that swell
shrunken bellies, smooth withered souls,
"Are you America?" each wary sojourner asks.
Soft pillows and ample blankets nestled deep in
    hammocks,
nightmares you help smother,
sweet dreams you set in motion,
"Are you?"
O, most wondrous throng—huddled masses—
it is you who are America! My America!

Ruth Sabath Rosenthal
New York City, New York

Winter Sunset

Under a St. Louis Bridge

Homeless man's eyes close;
He listens to a cricket,
Feels a hot breeze pass.

This soundless man's eyes open—
Taking a sip of noon sun.

Patrick T. Randolph
La Crosse, Wisconsin

Elder Park

Homeless words on
The Wind,

Gathering together
For warmth

Inside this old
Woman's ear.

Patrick T. Randolph
La Crosse, Wisconsin

Chicago Street Musician

The train gusts in
on a rush of wind and grating rails.
Doors slash back,
releasing a teeming torrent of commuters
that inundates Washington Street Subway Station.
Cascading down the stairwell rapids,
deluging the State Street pedestrian tunnel,
coursing away in merging currents…
a roiling river of humanity.

Plectrumed chords from a Spanish guitar,
dulcet tones of Southern singing,
emanate from somewhere
beyond a vanishing point.
Borne on fetid air and neon glare,
compelling strains of *Amazing Grace*
resonate down the taint of graffiti-glyphed walls
to the rhythm of a cadenced footstep beat.

A tattered troubadour greets all,
nod of head, irrepressible air.
Cadging sinners with his sacred songs,
his musical message strummed,
eyes singing lyrics, his lips repeat,
his smile, their meaning spoken:
"Step out of your worried little worlds,
your sad sequestered selves,
for we have but little time to laugh and love."
Dollars fall—a few fluttering leaves
into the cache of his battered guitar case.

Don Melcher
Merrillan, Wisconsin

46

Behind Bars

After Stevie Smith's [7] *"Parrot"*

Plucked from rainforest greenery,
the parrot was handed a *fait accompli:*
barred from flight, faced with scenery
far from agreeable—even remotely.

In a dank cage, barely a foot wide,
she withstood incarceration
for years—then snapped—
in the throes of raging self-pity—
She pecked her downy skin bloody;
beyond molten, clawed an eye out,

flung it to the dark hearth
in the rental on Central Park South;
then, with a swell of her aching chest,
opened herself to death.

Ruth Sabath Rosenthal
New York City, New York

---

[7] Stevie Smith (1902-1971) was an English poet and
novelist. She won the *Queen's Gold Medal for Poetry* in
1969.

Ides of March

Here—always—
Southside Chicago;
Prostitutes and recyclers,
Scrap-metal yards and newspapers in the wind;

Good wholesome poetry—every Goddamn where
    you look!

Wild dogs lunging off the morning railroad tracks,
Homeless man yawning,
Southside streets—
Always—alive!

Patrick T. Randolph
La Crosse, Wisconsin

Help!

I took Eva Skettle in
when she had no place to go.
She came out of the shelter,
said she's never going back.

I let her sleep on my couch,
gave her my old coat,
fed her. She helped
with the cleaning.

It's been four weeks—
Eva is a good person,
she needs a job, a place to stay.

She needs a new life—
I need my space!

Mary L. Downs
Appleton, Wisconsin

Man in a Cardboard Box

A shroud of sullen clouds
drapes the pinnacles of skyscrapers.
Dismal morning rain
drizzles into late afternoon.
Concrete along the affluent
LaSalle Street corridor
shimmers in abstract imagery,
portraying a surreal sense
of the City blustering
in a gyrating collage of confusion.

A tinge of Down Syndrome about his eyes,
bovine body hunched, dwarf legs splayed,
protruding feet shod in broken-down, unlaced
    shoes,
fingers dripping over a tin of spaghetti;
incongruous, he sits in a cardboard box.
Though deep in depths of other scenes,
he is not oblivious to disdainful stares:
repugnant nods, and mirthful mutterings
of the cortege of umbrella-dripping passersby—
dapper in Neiman Marcus business suits,
Marshall Field overcoats and Florsheim shoes.

Precariously close to the curb,
his sidewalk sanctuary is swamped
in a wake of breaking surf
from the regatta of rush-hour traffic.
The sad, sagging roof
deliquescing into papier-mâché
and sodden walls shedding corrugated scales
portend disastrous consequence.

A fish bone caught in the throat of society…
his persona asks perplexing questions:
"Who are the rich?" "Who are the poor?"
"Who the givers?" "Who the receivers?"
"Don't you see my gift?"

Don Melcher
Merrillan, Wisconsin

The Transitive Property
of Hunger

Through the hot callous dust
    of noisy Tijuana,
  we saw her up ahead of us
    in a sunbaked doorway—
baby on hip,
    bitter impatience in
        her eyes,
one hand out
    as we approached;

I gave a bit
    of what was
        needed—
with that, she turned and
    carried the baby
        and the humility
    around the corner.

A few doorways,
        corners later,
    out came the same hand
        and the downcast eyes—
    the baby stared blankly out
        into a future with
            and without food—

        and my stomach
                tightened.

Katrin Talbot
Madison, Wisconsin

Train Hopping

My brother hooks up with the train kids
who chase down the boxcars for rides,
bruised by the iron-rail life.

"I hate it, I hate it," one hisses,
"and what does it give back to me?
Black eye, broken ankle, burn scar,

missing teeth, nights spent around campfires,
liquid Colt 45, the limitlessness
of being outside—all the time."

With the doors of the boxcars wedged open,
they doze to the rhythm of the tracks,
but the noise of the train starts retreating,

falling back, though they're still on the train.
It's a hint of what dying will sound like—
the world's clatter fading away.

They are traveling up in the North now,
and I hope while they sleep it will snow,
so cool whiteness will fill all their wounds,

for the hum of a train fast receding
can sound like you're on your way home.

Michele Leavitt
Moscow, Idaho

Designer on the Street Corner

Like corrugated armor, his cardboard suit
protects him from the truth of his environment—
an ensemble of found fabrics designed
on the drawing board of his mind, assembled
on the only cutting table at hand—the city
    sidewalk.

The jacket impeccably cut from boxes
and artfully seamed with masking tape,
its "sleeves," and the "pants" beneath it—
paper bags in matching tones of tan
wrapped smartly around his arms and legs,

tucked into plastic bags covering his feet
like boots, not the black or white ones,
but grocery store beige ones, chosen
with his eye for color, to complement
the cardboard. He wears his whole creation

with the swagger of a runway model
and a proud toss of dreadlocks, as if to say,
"Had circumstances been a little different,
I'd have been shown in Paris, acclaimed
the toast of New York or the darling of Milan."

Gretchen Fletcher
Fort Lauderdale, Florida

54

Magical

I found a quarter the other day;
it seemed shinier than I remembered one to be,
it seemed rounder,
    newer,
    more brilliant.
I think it went up my nose
and out my mouth as a cigarette—
and God
was it good!

Denise Amodeo Miller
Buffalo, New York

O'

to be a man
                who accepts his fall

        as serenely

                        as autumn
leaves.

                                Kenneth P. Gurney
                        Albuquerque, New Mexico

At the Intake Desk

Behind the partition, they wait for their turns,
they wait to see me, to answer my questions,
to put problems into words, trusting that
I'll understand.

A child races about, ignores reprimands,
another needs a fresh diaper, a bath.
The unwanted teenager lacks a place to stay,
hopes to finish school, needs love.

One mother, shattered by a marital crisis,
requests rent money, emergency food to tide
her fatherless family over till AFDC or WIC[8]
takes effect.

The pale, recovering alcoholic is hungry,
needs gasoline to reach the job he just landed;
a job which may just put him back on his feet.

We are not their panacea—
with restricted funds, we may offer limited,
emergency help, make referrals, install a sense of
    hope.

I finger a blank application form, prepare to listen,
write the story without an ending.

Mary L. Downs
Appleton, Wisconsin

---

[8]AFDC (Aid to Families with Dependent Children) and
WIC (Women, Infants and Children) are two publicly
funded programs.

Alone and Hungry

When you're alone, short on money,
you worry about which bill you won't pay
so you can eat.

When you're alone, nobody knows
what's in your closed kitchen cabinet,
if there's anything there at all.

When you're alone, you don't feel guilty, just
    shame
while sneaking the last bag of stale chips
to nibble on like an animal.

When you're alone, you don't want people to
    know
what's not in your checking account—
except a few cents you can't buy anything with.

When you're alone, you worry about
writing on a piece of paper
that can't be backed up by cash,

But you're not alone when you feel
    embarrassment
for taking food from someone else
who needs it more than you.

June A. Thompson
Neillsville, Wisconsin

Evening Rounds

Mary's Place

Inside the city, Homeless find their way to Mary's
    Place:
a haven, an oasis for Their spirits
that seek the home within.
They are nameless, faceless, jobless,
searching for a place to call—home.

Inside the populace, They find themselves at
    Mary's Place:
a portal, warmth for Their souls,
searching for that one meal—a gift.
They find Their names, see Their faces, work at
    Their lives,
searching to fit inside—the world.

Inside the space, the Homeless find others'
    kindness—
cracked esteem, mapped lines on Their faces,
mending into a zigzag—a scar.
They begin to heal; Their wounds close, humbled
    spirits
searching for Their pride—forced into another
    way of living.

June A. Thompson
Neillsville, Wisconsin

60

Anna

If sturdy could be regal,
Anna would be queen of her whole world—
a realm of desperate women,
where stale bread fried in bacon grease
fills the bellies of a family
the last week of every month
and Kool-Aid fills the hunger that remains.

Some say she's too honest;
She shouts the F-word if it suits.
She gives food pantry rations
to others poorer than herself
when she has a little extra
and they don't, because she lived
for years with not enough.

She hugs her children often,
teaches them to share,
uses laughter and small smiles
to let them know that they are loved.
They understand that "making do"
is hard, know that "having" isn't all—
that "staying together" keeps them safe.

An oracle with street smarts,
Anna shares the best she has:
plainspoken words served
with flavored instant coffee,
lumpy cookies from the oven
that "never holds the heat"
and her sheltering arms
for anyone in need.

Lou Roach
Poynette, Wisconsin

Somewhere Downtown

Somewhere downtown
Loneliness walks the hurried streets of strangers,
Drifts amid the flux of cadenced footfalls,
Searching face to face, the guarded glances,
Some inter-spark of mutual acquaintance.

Indigence panhandles a pulsating street corner,
Chanting the mantra…"Hungry! Hungry!
    Hungry!"
Apathy passes by, heart averted,
Cold eyes fixed on some vague point of
    perspective.

Innocent's wide-eyed child—Curiosity's protégé—
Skips to the rhythm of a sidewalk cavalcade.
Enchanted by a street musician's jaunty airs,
Dances in the reflections of Fantasy's window
    world.

Somewhere downtown
Affluence struts to the gleam of a waiting limo,
Disdaining stares of the common passers-by,
Luxuriates in the wealth of superior status,
Perusing life through the tinted glass of plush
    backseats.

A street pastor preaches to a congregation of gray
    walls,
His rant echoing the self-righteous prophets of
    doom.
Drunkenness grovels in the debauch of dry gutters,
Addiction proselytizing a new generation of junkie.

Blindness, led by a cane, crosses the street,
Tapping a beat into the peril of teeming traffic.
Compassion, flouting danger sprints to the front,
Becoming his brother's eyes, his brother's keeper.

Somewhere downtown
Festoons of flowers bloom in the concrete garden,
Soft breezes primp their swaying petals.
A low sky touches the tops of jutting towers,
Sunlight sweeps the streets of lingering shadow.

Don Melcher
Merrillan, Wisconsin

Stealing Jesus

She lived alone on the streets,
so she lifted the six-foot tall
wooden Christ
weighing ninety pounds
off the front of the sanctuary.

Now *James the Less Church* is
more the less,
and Christ, too,
losing both previously scarred hands,
and a toe.

Educated in the Scriptures, she said,
"If God is with you,
who can be against you?"

She was jailed about 12:40 p.m., Sunday,
on suspicion of grand theft.
Officials believe the statue can be restored.

Mary Langer Thompson
Apple Valley, California

Backseat Reflections

In the vacated lot next to Henry's Garage,
    which doubles as a way station for stolen
    goods,

sits a two-door Toyota Corolla—
    no engine and the inside stripped.

On four cinderblocks, it is another eyesore
    in a bourgeoning community. In the backseat,

draped in a wool blanket handed out
    by the Catholic Worker on 13th and T Street,

is my damp body crumpled in a fetal position.
    Rain pummels the somber night nonstop.

Cold air occupies the wretchedness
    running through me. I reflect back

twenty years to a bedspread with NFL logos—
    wonder about the possibility of time travel.

Randall Horton
Albany, New York

Shopping List

I look to my left on this packed city bus—
Sitting next to me, a middle-aged homeless man
Writes a short list on a scrap of brown paper bag:
Comb, Finger Nail Clippers, Dr. Pepper.

He winks at me and smiles a story:
His yellowed teeth the color of August wheat,
His breath a strange mix of toothpaste and beer.
"Don't think I can buy all of 'em,
But writin' 'em down, ya see, keeps me thinkin'
    and plannin',
And my penmanship gets practice."

"That's right," I answer and point to a shiny nickel
In front of a businessman's black leather shoes.

I dig into my pockets—he stops me.
"Your smile is good, your eyes don't lie.
I think you'll change the world with them
Buckteeth of yours—that country boy grin.
Keep your coins, you've just given me
A nickel and…maybe a whole heck of a lot
    more."

Patrick T. Randolph
La Crosse, Wisconsin

66

Panhandler's Song

Her mantra— *"Spare a little*
change? Have a nice day."—a gift of music
to the song-less bustle of commuters and their
daily outpouring at the railhead.

A two-bar ditty laced with Calypsonian
optimism, percussed by the tambourine jingle
of her change cup, hopeful syncopation
given lie by mirthless eyes cast down
at scarred pavement, and then

the predictable coda *sans* conviction—
rush hour's desultory staccato
rhythms flattened out by the drone
of her cadenced intermezzo voiced
with metronomic precision.

Krikor N. Der Hohannesian
Medford, Massachusetts

Message on the Door

While driving past a mission
That serves the urban poor,
I saw a painted sign
Hanging on the door.

To me it was amusing,
Yet conveyed the message well:
A message of compassion,
A poet's privilege to tell.

For God so loves the humble
And the poor He won't ignore.
"Beans, Rice, and Jesus Christ"
Was the message on the door.

Liz Mastin
Coeur d'Alene, Idaho

Small Change

God stopped by
A church
The other day,

It stayed long
Enough
For *Her* to feel
Each member
Of the congregation
Feel *His*
Presence,

And then
It scooted up the street,
Filled with hot sun
And cool shadows,
To stand outside a small
Coffee shop
As a sad manifestation
Of a homeless woman
Happily wearing
Her old lover's
Oversized
Raincoat
With the hood pulled over
His face,
So you could only hear
Her voice
As *It* asked
For
Small change.

Patrick T. Randolph
La Crosse, Wisconsin

Home in the Wind

Human Economics

A homeless man on the street selling
Newspapers, [9]

His pockets bulging with more life
Than my own.

We look at each other, nod and exchange smiles:
Each of us understanding, knowing and accepting
Responsibility for the other's emotional well-being

Of being well and being kind;

Kind to our grins,
Kind to our eyes,
Kind to our moment together—

Passing each other's
Transparent miracle,
Here—on this shadowed South-Side street.

Patrick T. Randolph
La Crosse, Wisconsin

[9] There are currently 17 homeless street newspapers in
the United States and 78 worldwide.

ഇ **III** ൙

Each day is a journey
and the journey itself home.

Matsuo Basho:
Narrow Road to a Far Province

Through the Pines

Water on Stone

A continual dropping weareth away stone.
Solomon

In the hot shower I scrub my
skin pink. Earlier, shielded
from water at the bus stop, I wore
a hooded raincoat and boots.

A woman next to me, worn with age,
fouled rain-fresh air. Reeking of sweat,
her second pair of slacks peeked
from beneath the first,
three sweaters pulled over her sagging bosom,
and a moth-eaten shawl over all.

She cradled a brown grocery bag
filled with acrid-smelling garments,
and on her head she wore a yellow plastic
colander like a helmet for battle.

I edged away from the odors,
stifled the impulse to offer directions
to a shelter, or press some money
into her hand; instead I remained a cold,
wet stone on the windy street corner.

Helen Padway
Glendale, Wisconsin

Late Summer Falls

Just a Mom

She was young, maybe 19, and rather plain looking. She was dressed in jeans and an old army shirt; her hair was tied back in an amber ponytail; her face looked tired. I rang up her groceries, and she handed me a book of coupons issued by the welfare office. It was 1:30 a.m. on a Wednesday night...a slow time for 24/7 grocers. "I always shop at this time," she said. "No one I might know around to see me." I looked into her eyes and said "That's okay, Honey, no one really pays all that much attention." "No," she said "probably not, but I am trying to get through school and with two kids, it's not easy to make it without these." She glanced down at the coupons in her hands. She cringed. "Hey, don't you feel bad," I told her. "When you have that there degree, you can make it on your own; but for now that's what these things are for...just a little help over the rough spots. Come by during the day, sometime, there's nothing to be ashamed of. You hold that head of yours high. You are teaching your children a real lesson in survival...." And then she smiled. Tears filled her blue eyes...someone had seen her...had truly seen her.

Susan F. Kirch-Thibado
Menomonie, Wisconsin

75

Homeless Dancers

I saw two ragged men looking
as if they had been ground into the dirt;
their hair like tangled roots.
They were probably not as old as they looked;
the earth lined their faces.
They danced together, holding hands
with total abandon in front of a street
band on the corner of the city sidewalk.
They cheerfully ignored the indifference
of the clean and well-dressed
who walked sedately by, moving to
the same solemn music.

Nancy Gauquier
Santa Cruz, California

Mother and Child

This isn't a scene from Bethlehem, but
the cave is familiar with wisps

of straw scattered over the earthen floor.
The young mother is resting;

we cannot see her eyes.
She is watching the baby curled up

beside her, protected by her simple robes
and outstretched arm. The arm too thin,

the baby too still. No hovering father is here,
no adoring shepherd. They are gone—

swallowed up by rage and war,
for this is not Bethlehem—

this is Darfur;

and the mother is starving,
her baby is dead

and the wise men
too busy
to visit.

Kathleen H. Phillips
Waukesha, Wisconsin

A Change in Circumstances

Ironic, Tim never wanted to go to school,
a genius at creating excuses. These days,
he's understood that school has food.
Supper is usually late and light.
He told me some kids don't like
the almost warm pancakes and sausage
at breakfast, but they have butter AND syrup.
Even peas at lunch aren't so bad anymore.
Once he said his stomach felt just like
the tin man's in that book he'd read—hollow.

Ironic, I always did want to lose weight,
tried many diets, always had excuses.
These days, I'm glad I kept my size tens.
I work extra, earning more money
so supper is not always skimpy.
I brown bag it, try to cover necessities:
rent, heat, bus, clothes, electricity.
The car had to be sold awhile ago.
I tell Tim life is a roller coaster—
but we'll ride its ups and downs together.
Yes, that I assure him—always together.

Elda Lepak
Hendersonville, North Carolina

Clean Plate

"Finish your dinner!"
"Clean your plate!"
"Two more Brussels sprouts—
think of the starving people in India!"

I could never, ever,
scowl or roll my eyes—
my fork obedient
since I'd seen them
at a tender age—
the starving
in India.

I never understood how
my cleaned plate
could possibly help
the diet of starving Indians—
but whatever it took,
I'd do it at five
because of the memories
of dust, heat and thirst
and of sunken eyes and crying babes—
the desperate look
    of the hungry
and the hungry look
    of the desperate.

Katrin Talbot
Madison, Wisconsin

Precarious

I don't know how I will pay the rent,
or how long my stash of food will last,
or how I will pay for my next fix of Xanax.

I once saw a homeless old man
defecating in a trash can in New York City.

I have seen homeless old women
screaming obscenities as if they had escaped
from the *Wizard of Oz,*
homeless war veterans passed out drunk
on city sidewalks or in subway stations,
pants down, unconsciously mooning the passers-by.

I have seen runaways with kittens on leashes
and disheveled people with puppies
in shopping carts, lone women with cardboard signs
begging for mercy in the middle of traffic.

They embody my greatest fear,
a constant reminder of what could happen to me.

Nancy Gauquier
Santa Cruz, California

Mystery at Morning Symphony

Always a short, brown, sleeveless
polyester dress
trimmed in blue
that doesn't show wrinkles,
that's certainly true;
but does show wear
and a snag or two.

Ill-fitting shoes, un-socked
legs—goose bumped and chapped—
short gray hair
in slept-on style,
wrinkled bare arms
like a beige sweater
with sleeves un-darned.

Coatless, ticket in hand,
she stands
on cold winter mornings
and waits
for locked doors to open—
eager for rehearsal music—
warm, sun-golden.

I wonder where she spends her nights…
on a bench in the park?
Does morning's music memory
soften her soul in the dark?

Dorothy Stone
Concord, Massachusetts

Hunger

I hunger for light, alone
with cold in my pockets.
How deep now the snow
on these mean streets.
Even the silver moon fades,
enshrouded in clouds.
On this dark side of panes,
I am out of illumination.
Icicles reach down to me,
they comfort me—
proof of impermanence.

Linda Aschbrenner
Marshfield, Wisconsin

Open Eyes

Lost on a Journey to Nowhere

Too small I am
On this bulging earth. Flea on the back
Of an itching dog.
Fleeting thought through some busy brain.
Crouched beneath this breathing bridge.
Speck of tar on
Trucker's whirring wheel.
Around and around
I go.
Here
But not here, always there, out there, way out
     there
Beyond the Sight of Society.
Annoying blur on an ancient eyeball.
Wandering, always gone.
Frozen in the desert. Fog on a mirror
That ripples like a river's song.
Crusty skin rubbing against
This prairie town's oozing bruise.
Lost on a journey to Nowhere.

                    Larry Wahler
                    Roscoe, Illinois

Late October Evening

Tonight when I stop to listen
everything starts to move around me.

When I stand before the black forest
and stare up,
I stumble from the stars.

The night is a kind witch
who charms us
with her sparkling sky of wine.

It is harvest time
and the melon of the moon
hangs ripe among
the creeping vines of clouds.

Rapture is the crunching of leaves,
the snapping of sticks
when only the wind is out there walking.

Scott J. Brooks
Omro, Wisconsin

Forest Voices

Cardboard box
from the homeless shelter,
now an alley condo.

✳

Flat tire pillow,
torn upholstery blanket
comfort a car trunk kid.

✳

Zooming train,
Affordable housing—
for homeless faces.

✳

Homeless temp worker
recalls that campfire pot roast
in this warm diner.

David S. Pointer
Murfreesboro, Tennessee

Recognize Him

His face is encrusted with dirt, his white
Hair unkempt. He shuffles down the street,
Carrying one old suitcase and his plight—
He has nowhere to go, no one to meet.

After twenty-five years, the company
Folded—just in time to take his pension;
The house that belonged to his family
For years received little attention

From the highway planning board. Stripped of all
But this pride, he walks through the park where
      his dear
Grandchildren play. They laugh, jeer, and call
Him names—not recognizing him this year.

Deborah Hauser
Babylon, New York

Poverty Grants the Exclusive

Poverty
states that he enjoys Macanudo
cigars, Moonlite BBQ, and Sonoma
County Chardonnay, but is
especially fond of children's
inner spirits which he nibbles
like edible plants with a
little roasted corn puree
as an added ingredient.
Poverty confesses that when
dining with his partner's
international businessmen, he enjoys
Ruppe's mussels in bagna cauda
with American asparagus sauce.
Poverty also cites American
plainclothes professors who
have infiltrated spoken word
speakeasies and academic
journals in order to corral
subject matter into a few
authorized areas as being a
great source of inspiration
to him. He also recalls that in his
childhood drive-by bullets
were often the first performance
enhancers offered to preadolescent
athletes before moving on to
amphetamines, steroids, and other
substances. Yes, this
has been a great life, indeed.
As a younger, yet fully developed
concept of human construct, Poverty
went hunting often with his founding

stepfathers, and field dressed
Social Justice, only to stand in front
of her with a first aid kit when
mixed media arrived with their cameras.

Poverty regrets that he doesn't
publish as much as he used to due
to more pressing concerns such as
shutting down young writers' inner
spirits so that Hope's wire service
is never up and running smoothly;
and when he can take time away
from building the global economy,
Poverty can be found almost anywhere
pushing the heart's heavy
boulders onto whole communities
like Xenophon's army in repeat retreat.
He concludes by stating that he
hopes to see you soon in a Midwestern
housing project, an Indian reservation,
Costa Rica, Peru or somewhere, so he
can share his unpretentious optimism
over some Ligurian cuisine and a
single serving of Glenfiddich Scotch
whiskey, topped off by Tea Anemone
with the special orange or Chrysanthemum
blossoms that burst lavishly open
as they steep while you enjoy your
government issued commodities
that have been so lovingly provided.

David S. Pointer
Murfreesboro, Tennessee

He No Longer Cares for Sex

Cedric chants spiritual poetry for a living.
He lived under the steel bridge,
lice and mange overcame his chin.

The river is pink and cloudy.
Semis on the bridge look like toys from the grass.
A long time from here, sat a girl in tennies and her
    favorite t-shirt.
Cedric would have been around 30, on crack.

Here, the bridge has a strong backbone, its spine
    uncracked.
There have been weaker spines.

He's not religious. His wife wanted him to be.
She's going through the change. She wants him back,
now that he's *making money* and moving to L.A.

Once he was given 10 twenties.
He bought a winter coat and supplies and gave a
    couple bucks to his friend, Skip,
because one should take care of the poor.
His wife is vain. Her beauty is outer, Cedric's is in
    deep hibernation.

"Cedric," said God, "Cedric, don't go back to your wife."
He restocks supplies for lice control when he can,
    trusts God.

When he took the 46 pain pills, he woke with
    them coming out
his bowels and throat. He no longer cares for sex.
There is something wrong with his kidneys.

Death is the cure for desire,
waking is the root of all suffering.

Homeless is like a job, requires training. His spine
    won't crack.
He writes a new name in his prayer book daily,
    something all should keep,
like his sister's; she married a hard Muslim from
    Africa.
Desire is directional. Cars driving the steel bridge
usually accept the road
rather than plunge into the river. Once in awhile
there is a collision.

Naomi Fast
Portland, Oregon

Man About Town

His stride was a study in meter
and any female looking his way
from the *Leaf and Bean*
as he crossed the street
would become an immediate student

Black leather blazer
body cigar straight in blue jeans
tucked into boots
dark hair growing out of his halfway
unbuttoned tan shirt
two day stubble and longhair look
of a GQ model

Five sips of coffee later I look up
and he's ransacking
the four trash cans out front
toasting other people's excess
with paper cups
In moves fluid as the lattes
chai and chocolate milk
slide down his throat

He's become a fine wine connoisseur
who couldn't be bothered to replace
hiking boots with soles wallet thin
whose domestic help forgot to hem
the lining that hangs below black leather
or wash the once white shirt
that wears the foods he's been scavenging

Now he's the city sanitation engineer
conducting a field study

Empty Shoes

who sets aside samples of pizza
submarine sandwiches and chicken wing bones
scoops it all with bureaucratic certainty
into a threadbare backpack
and not one of us watching
wishes to humble him
with the truth of a handout

Ellaraine Lockie
Sunnyvale, California

Lottie

Lottie walked into my life: a fifty-five-year-old
woman I scarcely knew, she lived
down the road with an older man for twenty-some
years but never married. He kept his job
at the foundry; she did the cooking, washed the
    clothes.

He gave Lottie money for trinkets, took her
to a tavern Friday nights for fish,
to a movie now and then at the Drive-In.
When she came to tell me that he was moving out,
she said he didn't ask her to come along, nor did he
seem concerned about her.

I read it all in Lottie's face: the hurt and helplessness,
the soul-searching—"What had I done wrong?"
"How can this be happening to me?"

I felt the catch in her throat, felt her stifled sobs
at the shock of being alone: no family, no work
    experience,
no income, no savings.

I picked up her suitcase, carried it to the spare
    bedroom.
"Let's have some coffee," I said. "You can rest
    later."

Mary L. Downs
Appleton, Wisconsin

Corn Story

I drop my box of produce at the shelter,
peering inside to dark rooms.
Corn, tomatoes, squash and peppers
glow like gems encrusted on a crucifix
in a California mission.

People huddle on the sidewalk,
stringy hair, squinty eyes,
lives reduced to backpacks—
like pictures I've seen of
the Santee Sioux at Fort Snelling—
bodies wrapped in smallpox blankets
asleep in damp pens.

At crowded tables
they eat sun-filled kernels once picked by priests,
ears twisted off with a creaky groan,
leaving tassel-headed skeletons
to mourn their empty stalks.

Jan Chronister
Maple, Wisconsin

Hard Times

Turkey

Thanksgiving, Elmhurst subway station

As I exit the G train,
I pass a man sitting on a wooden bench;
his lanky bronze hair
hangs like a worn Olympic ribbon,
his long yellow fingers
rubbing the corners of a newspaper.
His shirt is neat yet worn with
faded splotches.
Twelve gray, shredded plastic bags
sit in neat, pressed rows of 4 abreast, 3 across—
they are filled with more neatly folded, pressed
dirty plastic bags.

The line of his nose is long, noble
like the tip of a sword,
his neck bent forward
like a knight who sips deeply of the grail before it
      vanishes,
his fingers rubbing circles around and around the
      newsprint
that is the color of a peeled, old potato.
His eyes lowered to last month's headlines:
      ROBBERY IN JAMAICA,
carefully studying each word like it is the Magna
      Carta—
as if he is interested, as if he is engaged,
as if he has something he is happy doing.
His loneliness is palpable,
it hungers for love,
its light falls
through the glow of fluorescent ceiling tubes,

98

his soul is shining,
spreading a sheen on the movie posters,
glossing the streaked porcelain tiles of the tunnel
    walls.

On my way up grimy stairs
toward a warm winter night
and drizzling air,
I stop and give thanks
for all that I have.

Before
entering a toasty ground-floor apartment
with warm, ritual embraces
and too much rich, good food,
before my tongue is slurred with gravy,
I close my wet, tearing eyes:
"Please, God, hear me—
give this man a good life,
please, for the rest of his life,
please, this one time God, just once, please,
a miracle,
some happiness—
some turkey."

Clara Sala
New York City, New York

The Bracelet

Two years ago
today
I touched your face
for the last time,
your skin
still soft and warm
with that lone
sigh.

I unfastened
the magnetic bracelet
from your wrist,
the one we thought
might cure you,
and put it on.
I never guessed
it was to heal me.
I didn't know then
your absence would
make me homeless—
or that grief,
like silently falling
snow, would bury
and unshape my
landscape.

It's been two years, Mom,
and I still wear
the bracelet.
The drifts shift,
a hint of my heart
song returns. Still,
the rawness bites

and seeps into
the cracks when
I least expect it.
It's then I hear
your voice,
the one that called me
"Joey."

Mary Jo Balistreri
Waukesha, Wisconsin

On Being Homeless

Am I
Houseless? Yes!
Apartment-less? Yes!
Motel-less? Yes!
Shelter-less? Yes!
Shack-less? Yes!

Am I
Homeless? No!

I live inside God—
And the rooms are large enough
In this world-mansion structure to stretch my
    legs—

And, of course, if I like,
To stretch my soul as far as the Spirit's echoed
    laughter!

Patrick T. Randolph
La Crosse, Wisconsin

Alley Row

Cardboard box,

   Mansion bliss—

      Roof leaks a bit.

     Patrick T. Randolph
     La Crosse, Wisconsin

Old Ben's Accordion

Shopping cart's
       Squeaky song—
              Hitting high notes.

          Patrick T. Randolph
          La Crosse, Wisconsin

Vic's Blessing

Miracle,
      Eyes open—
            Gift of new day.

                        Patrick T. Randolph
                        La Crosse, Wisconsin

Which Side of the Table?

I was pouring milk as fast as I could.
There must have been at least
a hundred and fifty
in the soup kitchen line that cold day.

The woman to my left
was dishing out brownies,
while the man to my right
handled the big coffee urn.

We had to wear thin plastic gloves
and cover our hair when we served,
as if the homeless people
gave a damn.

I was wearing my blue Navy cap
with the name, *Shipley Bay,*
tattooed on it,
CVE-85. [10]

Some carried all their possessions
in black plastic bags,
others carried them under their arms
and smelled like the clothes
they slept in.

Finally, when we were nearly through,
people started coming back
for seconds.

---

[10] The *USS Shipley Bay (CVE-85)* was a *Casablanca*-class
escort carrier of the United States Navy. *Shipley Bay* was
awarded two battle stars for her World War II service.

An old guy hesitated in front of me,
but didn't want anything.

"I saw your ship at Iwo," he said.
It took me aback,
I wasn't certain of what he said,
"I saw your ship at Iwo," he repeated.

"Were you in the Navy?" I asked.

"No," he answered. "I was with the 28th
    Regiment."

"I heard your outfit was among the first to land,"
    I said.

"Did you watch us go ashore?"

"No, we were too far offshore. Did you watch
the flag go up on Suribachi?"

"I watched it go up from the hospital ship."
He holds up his right hand with two fingers
    missing.

"You're lucky to be here," I said.

"You think so?"

I knew what he meant...
he was on the wrong side of the table,
carrying everything he owned
in a black plastic bag.

Bruce Muench
Roscoe, Illinois

ೞ **IV** ೞ

The gentleman seeks neither a full
belly nor a comfortable home. He is
quick in action but cautious in speech.

Confucius: The Analects, *Book I*

Last-Chance Motel

Gone Without a Trace

When the shelter released its homeless flock
  before dawn, nobody street-ridden realized
Crip vanished from the city's architecture,
  his body imprint no longer an outline.

Usually, in daybreak mist, (and this was
  his modus operandi) Crip could be observed
struggling down Q Street, backpack slung over
  his left shoulder, dragging a shriveled right leg,

which was a kickstand to balance
  the rest of his stocky frame, hence the name
Crip. From the Midwest, St. Louis, to be exact,
  he wore a dress uniform of green camouflage,

aware that every day was Berlin, Korea,
  Vietnam, Desert Storm. Walking 45 degree
angled against morning traffic, his combat
  boots spit-shined into mirrors—

Crip knew the soft edges of the streets,
  how to tightrope danger without
ever leaving the neighborhood, a high-wire act
  perfected by years of survival.

At the free-food table in the northwestern
    corridor,
  before eggs and oatmeal waft the air,
no one gives a second thought to the nonexistence
  of the would-be Green Beret with a slight drawl.

His limp, or lack of it, will leave no recollection
  on 14th Street where he leaned, only yesterday,
on the side of a laundromat, his tired frame
  to the incessant drone of rush-hour traffic.

Randall Horton
Albany, New York

Keeping Watch

Petit Déjeuner[11]

Plain burning croissant on a
cold metal plate—

Can hunger tell me
which is which?

Greta Aart
Paris, France

---

[11] *Petit déjeuner* is French for *breakfast*. In France it
usually includes juice, coffee or tea, and a roll.

Soup

Small bowl filled with noodles
floating in a little yellow sea;
sometimes the warmth of you is too good—
more than one can bear,
pushing love inside my belly
without my consent,
yet I'm lost in your moment
which awakens soft chimes in my gut
and calls the night open
to possibilities.

Denise Amodeo Miller
Buffalo, New York

Street Worship

"Do you have any advice for me?"
The man asked the sidewalk
very politely, his words eloquent.

"How should I behave to get into
or near Heaven?"
The man asked a streetlamp.

"How will I find a love
that will not cut out my heart?"
The man asked a discarded shopping cart.

Only the streetlamp answered,
and that was a hesitant flicker—
as if attempting to answer a prayer.

J. J. Steinfeld
Prince Edward Island, Canada

Shopping Cart Village

Hunger Disappearing in U.S.

Rocks in the water don't know the misery of rocks in the sun.
Haitian proverb

After a six-year rise, hunger fell in 2005 to only 35 million. In 2004, 38 million people were hungry. However, since 2006, it is no longer called "hunger." Nearly eleven million have "very low food security"—the worst category of gnawing in the belly. Twenty-four million only have "low food security"—a lesser form of insecurity, or better security. "Low food security" replaces "food insecurity without hunger," and "very low food security" replaces "food insecurity with hunger"—changes announced by the USDA at their weekly dinner meeting held at the Cheesecake Factory.

Judy Kolosso
Slinger, Wisconsin

Nocturne

I can hear him outside
the bar just before dawn,
hear him long before I can
see him pushing his home-
made cart, riding on the rims
of bicycle wheels, making
a god-awful noise with each
crack crossed, each indentation
raised by roots, each pitted
imperfection of the sidewalk,
until he stops to inspect
the garbage for deposit
bottles, the cart near to over-
flowing in this Gold Rush ghetto
of cast-off containers from students
and their friends, all weekend,
every weekend, one long floating
party from one house to the next,
all three floors of every walkup
brownstone an occupancy code
violation waiting to be discovered,
all of them drinkers, all of them
leaving their bottles and cans
for this Pied Piper of Western
Avenue serenading the "hood,"
rolling in cash collected, one nickel
at a time.

Alan Catlin
Schenectady, New York

Dupont Circle, Washington DC[12]

Where affluent young misses aim to please,
and messenger cyclists take their briefest ease,

and elderly and just-wed couples stride
past parents pushing strollers filled with pride,

dog walkers with their purebreds promenade
as rollerblading youth to iPods nod.

The fountain pours its incandescent splash
as cross their checked fields lightning chess pros flash,

and business moguls grab a power bite
by chalk protesters aching for a fight,

and students soak in the last October sun
as round about the cars and busses run.

While teeming streams of stubborn taxis churn
and diplomats in endless circles turn…

the homeless take curved benches for their bed,
and surround themselves with pigeons—better fed.

M. Lee Alexander
Williamsburg, Virginia

---

[12] Dupont Circle is widely known as a famous traffic
circle and historic district in Northwest Washington,
D.C. It is also known for its large homeless population.

Early Spring Snow

It Could Happen to You

I have no worries about taxes,
mortgages, house cleaning.
I walk a lot, get fresh-air exercise
each day—and some nights.
I also have no job, no house,
no car, no credit cards.
It seems as though I am stuck
in a weird parallel world.
I'd cry but need the time
to learn to live in my own city
all over again—from the inside.
Fourth Street Restaurant will give
handouts after hours—problematic
as shelters have an early check-in.
The soup kitchen is a godsend—
when there is enough for everyone.
The Texaco Station on Tenth allows
use of their restroom if I don't loiter.
The hardest part is keeping clean—
finding food,
    and wondering why I am here
    and how I can get out.

Elda Lepak
Hendersonville, North Carolina

119

Soul Music

Jim Bean, homeless poet veteran, calls to me like a
  prophet
from the side of the New Mexican trail. I turn at
  the sound
of his burning words falling like soul fire on solid
  ground.
"Lady, not many are like you. You need to know
  that, lady."
Jim Bean and I just talked eye to eye of poetry,
  Boston, God,
and the war. Some inner music harmonized, we
  danced,
shook hands, skin to skin in a real experience. I
  feel blessed
and confused by his emphasis. "You need to
  know that, lady."

The veteran bullshit detector, Dick, three-tour
  Navy medic friend,
says of my dream of making love with a famous poet,
"It's alright to have a projection, but if you keep it,
  it's a failure
of courage to be present to who is really there, not
  you or him,
I mean the energy that writes it all."

In the San Francisco tenderloin, Mark comes up
  asking for money.
I don't have any. He starts singing to me, a blues
  love song.
I start doing backup as he takes my arm in his
  beautiful ebony arm,
his deep yellow eyes shining like suns. We stroll
  Market Street singing,

stop in the park where he tenderly shows me
    pictures of his children
he never sees, talks of the war, the possibility of work,
until the dope woman comes by holding a raised
    hand like it was full of gold.
Mark takes my hand, saying he can't, he can't,
    until I cannot see him
for the crowd presses in, I only feel his grip on my
    hand until he lets go.

Sitting on the Washington DC sidewalk eating
    lunch with Tyrone Young
of the 96th Screaming Eagles, 101st Division, I
    get up to leave.
He takes my hand. "I want you to know I love
    you," he says,
"not because you got me a sandwich but because
    you just are."

Some stories plainly write themselves. In the old
    Irish myth,
the sea god made a bag of letters to hold the
    universe
from a crane woman's skin. In this spelling of the
    world, the language
of touch is the soul's tongue, a hand on hand, arm
    pressed against arm,
the feel of words penned in soul blood, words that
    are worlds—
Jim, Dick, Mark, Tyrone.

In memory, my fingers trace the touch of their skin
to feel the mysterious space between the letters.
Alone and leaning forward, I listen again for the song.

Barbara Flaherty
Columbus, New Mexico

121

La Bohème at the Lyric Again

At least three times before,
I have heard Left Bank conversation,
watched stage snow fall,
hoped Rodolfo would return to love anew,
watched Mimi cough, weaken, die.

Tonight again I will mourn
her needless death
while on nearby Chicago streets
artists still struggle to survive,
homeless children shiver,
men and women look in vain for work,
go hungry to their beds,
or light fires beneath viaducts
to gather warmth against the cold
until it takes their lives.

Wilda Morris
Bolingbrook, Illinois

Tsigan: The Gypsy Poem[13]

What if you lived in a box, in a tree, in a car by the
side of the road? What if your shoes were full of
rain and mud and you stank like the dog you
loved? What if you slept every night in a different
ditch, were always cold? What if you had no coat
but the coat you'd stolen, rag and wind?

What if you moved to keep warm and kept warm
by burning what you had? What if you bathed in
poisoned rivers, drank from them, ate their fish?
What if you crossed at dusk into a country
clamping down? What if they called you *gypsy*,
nomad, meant: *not wanted here*? What if they tried to
wipe you like a dark stain from the map? What if
you lived in a tree, a box, a car? What if you lived?

Cecilia Woloch
San Diego, California

---

[13] This poem is taken from the series of poems in the
collection *Tsigan: The Gypsy Poem* published by
Cahuenga Press, 2002.

House Keeping

The Shopping Cart Estates

We went to the park around
    the corner from the Academy
to lose ourselves in the mysteries
    of the banyan trees,

and there they were...
    the dark mysteries of society,
    the no-income versions
      of white picket fences,
    the quilts, the threadbare yards
   beneath the loaded shopping carts.

The boys under the biggest banyan,
  keeping afloat beneath the roots
    by a sweet morning
        drug deal,

and on the busy street corner
    of the park,
  beneath the extravagant
      tree canopy,
 she swept and swept
    her cardboard floors—
  empty shoes holding down
    the corrugated claim,
  her shopping cart
     containing the possibility of
      a life,
  her closet, her kitchen.

We walked back to
    the dress rehearsal,
leaving the transient lives

Empty Shoes

to float beneath
the comfort of the
ancient trees,
and the stunning
absurdity of their
desperate
roots.

Katrin Talbot
Madison, Wisconsin

Our Dissolving Histories

I used to live on the street, but it's difficult for me to say how long. Years, perhaps. It's not that I'm ashamed of that period of my life, but I don't know how to explain or justify it. Now I'm clean at least, a not-too-wrinkled suit of clothes, and I'm sitting here in one of the nicer parks in the city. It's a half-decent day. I can think, I can remember, I can look around me, and I have someone nearby—a longtime companion, even though he's reluctant to reveal his name. I am more talkative, but he is just as observant as I am. I've made an attempt at a writer's life; at least I have the memory of having been a writer.

We sit together on this park bench, interfering with no one, knowing only each other and what chances before our bench confined view. What loyal partners we have become, old, melancholy colleagues passing time, combing each other's hair as it falls out in unsightly protest, befouling our personal museums.

No new topics today, so we revise the old ones. We fight with imaginary gods as the real One shuns us so, save for the occasional pinch or jab or slap to make us pay for our fantasies, for our indefensibly lovely days, we still welcome our random punishments, gawking at the loveliness.

Soon it will be morning. We argue over the month but accept the tottering minute too enchanting to contest; we never have nor ever will comprehend the need for godliness. An unknown stray dog passes, depositing its indifference. We spit and pray without even budging the earth; we resort to lies to rearrange our sprawling futility—nearly victorious with our language.

If only we had the dog's courage instead of our landlocked stupidity, we could flee the park bench, float through the world we only hear of from rumors formed by the lips of mischievous winds.

We exchange the vast for the wasted, wasteful with our dreams, raising eyebrows to restore movement, praising oldness to restyle agedness. You and I have no laudable repute, no manner worthy of public presentation or a young woman's earnest sigh.

So long we have thought what refuses to exist; we are linked to ludicrousness, wondering what we have to hide, hiding what we wonder about. No comely answer, no shape sufficient, to save our dissolving histories—only the unknown is adequate.

In *your* boredom, I cut my wrists to test my hidden blood. You, park bench partner, bloodless and curious beyond compassion, question why I don't prick a finger to seek the ravishing color. I laugh and continue to bleed—what sordid sense of victory, what maniac's fluttering haughtiness as I hide in artfulness, preparing my reddened memories.

Soon you will be alone, your amusement
thwarted, dying unaccompanied. You say nothing
to that, you only act as I act—damn you, my
darker glow, my haunting essence, my mocking
beloved shadow.

J. J. Steinfeld
Prince Edward Island, Canada

Park Lady

To go from a slope of black dirt
to waiting brown water
is her objective—
a bath in wintry Central Park.
The pond beckons with its city ducks
and nautical sewer rats.
The place is better than nothing.

She doesn't bother to undress.
She lets the plastic garbage bags she has patiently
fashioned into blouse and skirt
bell around her like a nimbus,
lets the paper bags she uses for shoes
soak and tear in the pond's moist throat.

After her dip, she will rest,
lounge upon boulders west of the water;
she will pat herself dry
before a dinner party—with the pigeons.

Austin Alexis
New York City, New York

Throwaway

Who'll show her where to go tonight
when all the warm stores shut their doors?
When all the walkways roll up tight,
who'll show her where to go tonight?

She's being baptized by the streetlight;
her heroines will be the whores
who'll show her where to go tonight—
when all the warm stores shut their doors.

Laura Heidy-Halberstein
Alexandria, Virginia

We Must Away

Let us run off,
take the Orient Express,
ride the rails to some
city whose name we
can't pronounce,
in a country where
we don't speak
the language, and
girls wear red ribbons
only for the color.

Kenneth P. Gurney
Albuquerque, New Mexico

Street Scene

Tonight the Key West winds
swirl along the curb;
dried fronds whirl into restaurant doorways
and onto the porch of Veteran's Hall.

He sets up for the night
        in the entrance of an upscale boutique,
        an indented walkway
        just long enough to hold
        his sleeping body.
        Showcases of glittering jewels
        protected by iron bars create
        walls of shelter,
        the wind plays with the cardboard
        he props across the entryway.

What story does he carry
in his worn blue pack?
Who waits for him to come home
in night's dark memory?
When will he be whole again?
When will the bombs of his war
be silent?

                              Janet Leahy
                    New Berlin, Wisconsin

133

These Women

They do it for themselves—
these women wearing sheer stockings,
shoes dusted
with rubble that have been
their stoves, bookshelves, booties
crocheted for sons, daughters
now dead
in rubble they walk through.
These women in shoes dusted off
and stockings, carrying their lives
in sheets they once pressed crisp,
flung across a wedding bed,
memories of their first night still bright
in their minds—
they cling to scalloped sheets
in their hands;
cling to a community of souls, each
reaching deep down
in a way they never knew
was in them, could ever know
was possible, like
their universe gone in a gulp, but
not the bed's memories or
laughter over tables set with "good china,"
filled with hot bread, lentil soup, garlic like
a sweet drug, strong but not strong enough.

These women walk, have been walking
through centuries, through streets,
over mountains, across deserts, hiding, while
feeding infants from breasts
in name only; these women remember
giddy gossip, remember

where they hid
birthday cakes to surprise the innocent.

They are walking still,
caring for their last pair of stockings, as
one covets a scrap of love letter, the rest
lost in a fire or flood or who knows where.
They covet this luxury not out of vanity, but
for love
of the lost, for sanity, for hope
no matter how sheer, sheerer even
than the air they now breathe.

These stockings, not good for anything, really,
not good for holding water to bolster
a sinking roof or heart.
Still, these women, with
faces no longer pink, but
gray with shadow,
dust off their shoes—
slip on their stockings.

Madeleine Beckman
New York City, New York

In Front of the Liquor Store

"What's wrong?" I asked the frightened man
standing in front of the liquor store,
awaiting the briefest of releases
from his daily prison of despair.

While I was stumbling,
as is my common form of movement,
I bumped into a "something"
that I am sure was beyond human—
I won't say God, I never say God
unless I've had a half bottle or more—
and I forgot to say "Excuse me"
or "I'm sorry"
and the Divine was just as penniless as me.

J. J. Steinfeld
Prince Edward Island, Canada

Finding the Way

Assumptions

You move
along the sidewalk
pushing a cart
with all your belongings:

Only a thin white blanket
lying tangled
within the basket
and twice-crumpled newspaper.

What do I assume about you?

You pass by
the restaurant window
and stop to rest
from your labor,

pull the blanket free
to wrap it around your shoulders;
and the newspaper
flies up and into the traffic.

You watch it go
with resolute
sadness
in your eyes.

What do I assume about you?

I assume

this night
your sleep
will be a little colder;

I assume
the dark will be lonelier
without the whisper of words
against your skin.

Pamela Olson
Tuscaloosa, Alabama

Endless Vision

Grandma's House

My dad's mom runs a hotel south of the canal,
A cheap SRO in the middle of the block between
    the pool hall
and the Jesus mission where the open door reveals
rows of stoic men slumped in folding chairs
    pretending to listen
to the preacher and waiting, waiting for a chance
    to sleep
on one of the iron beds lined up like soldiers with
    white sheets pulled drum tight.

My mom parks our two-tone blue Pontiac outside
    the liquor store
stocked with amber pints of brandy, port, and
    muscatel.
She checks her lipstick in the rearview mirror.
She makes sure her stocking seams are straight
and my ponytail is so tight it makes my scalp ache.
She makes a beeline down the vomit-splattered
    street to Grandma's hotel,
past the broken men in broken shoes, in pants tied
    up with rope.
She does not look at the Army-green trouser leg
    neatly folded,
safety-pinned, and dangling slackly where a limb
    should be.
She's blind to the gap-toothed, yellowing ivories,
    the gray stubble lined with spittle,
the passed-out drunk lying twisted on the ground
    just as he fell,
wreathed in the sweet, stale fumes of cheap wine.

"Single Rooms • Daily • Weekly • Monthly"
　　reads the sign on *Baachan's*[14] hotel.
The door is checked and chalky with age and the
　　entrance reeks of piss.
"Don't touch the walls," my mother says. She
　　gathers her skirt tightly,
so it will not brush the stamped metal wainscoting
painted institutional green and stained with grease
　　from many hands.

Baachan is waiting for us at the top of the stairs,
at the end of a dim hall lined with bleak single rooms.
A tiny woman, skinny as the broom she wields,
as crooked as the teeth jammed any which way
　　into her mouth.

"*Yokatta, ne!*[15]" she sings when she sees us.
"*Namu Amida Butsu,* I pay homage to the
　　Buddha," she says.
And as she beams, it IS good. All of it—the ten
　　kids she raised in this skid-row hotel,
the drunks, the deadbeats, the bums who call her
　　"Mama" and eat her free Sunday chili,
a young nervous mother and a little girl with eyes
　　like cameras.
Nothing escapes the embrace of *Baachan*'s
　　compassionate view.

Going to see her is like visiting the sun.

Shizue Seigel
San Francisco, California

---

[14] *Baachan* is Japanese for *grandma*.
[15] *Yokatta, ne* literally means *It's good, isn't it*, however, in
this context, the meaning is closer to *It's good to see you*,
or *I'm happy to see you.*

142

The Prisoner

Double chain link topped with glistening razor
    wire,
the clank and screech of gates dragging,
and then the huge black man being led out to the
    yard,
one of many in a hidden human trap.

Hands in the pockets of his old Navy coat,
black knit hat rolled down over ears and brows,
a man searching for invisibility, too late.

We sit together on an iron bench under
the blue Nevada sky in eighty degrees.
Other black knit caps pass us covering
other heads, eyes sneaking a look.

The man is not sure why he is here,
or even where he is, or the name of his lawyer.
The lawyer does not know why this man is in
    prison.
The man says no one here knows much.

He was in a bar, a man was shot.
This man was not accused, he was just there.
Sometimes there can be mystery
about the obvious.

I arrange for his transfer to the hospital.
We will tell the court who he is,
but we will never be able to tell him that.

Many simple tasks are too difficult to do.

Empty Shoes

He will go home to nowhere,
a desert village where he spent his life,
doing nothing in particular.
Odd jobs, hanging out, waiting for nothing.
He is not crazy, or bad, or mean.
At home, in his village, he is invisible.
He knows right from wrong.
He knows to be invisible.
He will work harder at that now.

Julian I. Taber
Coupeville, Washington

Hard Times

When I worked, I bought some extra food,
tossed cans of beans, Spaghetti-O's,
into the cart beside the steak for Bob,
then left it in the box at church
where someone took it to the poor.
I never thought about it twice
or wondered who might need it,
and if they'd rather have
something tastier than what I gave,
fruit salad maybe, chicken breasts, fresh meat,
but no, spaghetti and beans would have to do.

Now Bob is gone—"passed on," some say.
They fancy it up, afraid to say the word.
He is DEAD and I'm alone.
The car is as creaky as me.
We both need work.
The garage makes no favors for old folks
nor the drugstore for the pills doc says I need.
My old coat will go another winter,
got no choice there.
But no matter how I stretch it,
there isn't much for food.

I'll have to use the food pantry.
Never did that before.
I wonder if you call ahead
or just show up.
What if my old friends see me
or Pastor John finds out?

Maybe I'll wait 'til later on
just before they close
when it's getting dark.

Judy Roy
Baileys Harbor, Wisconsin

I Hope It Will Do

I know
it is only a
poem. Spring

brings the
yellow crocus
and only this—some

grubby words. But I
made it for
you—and I hope it will do.

Joshua Moses
New York City, New York

God Won't Deal Man a Bad Hand

The morning shines brightly,
Warming my chilled bones
And I am at peace
In a positive world.
Circling above me,
A bird merry-go-round,
Their pipe-organ cantos—
A twittering song.
And the hazy half sky
That meets the horizon
Shines down its own song
In celebrating theme,
For life is perceived
In many ways but should
Be enjoyed for great beauty—
It's all very good.
Look at the transient
I sat by at Starbucks,
Sitting there mumbling
Soft words to himself,
Ragged and homeless
As he simply sought
Some short-term shelter
On Pike Street—alone.
Just a brief hello
I offered this poor man
With his beard and old clothes,
Long arms and frayed coat.
Then slowly and calmly
As sweet as a fresh lamb,
He turned to me and said
"God won't deal man a bad hand."

Liz Mastin
Coeur d'Alene, Idaho

The City of Chicago's
Concrete Concerto

He has a black, Greek ship-captain's hat
And a red long-sleeve shirt and black pants.
He sits stooped on a fire hydrant
By the Corner Bakery at Erie and St. Clair—
He calls out, "Help for the homeless"
At regular intervals.
All the brunch customers coming
From the restaurant and patio tables
In the mid-morning sunshine
Pass him by with indifference.
Vehicle traffic moves by the intersection
With a few muted horns sounding.
No sound of coins changing hands.
The forgotten homeless man's solo
Goes unacknowledged.
Suddenly, the whir and whine of a crescendo—
Construction equipment and high-rise building
    machines
Creates a chaotic din that drowns out the plaintive
    destitute one.
The chronic complaint of the homeless individual
Is masked by the mechanical musical marvels
Of Chicago's hardhatted concrete concerto!

John J. Quirk
Chicago, Illinois

Sad Streets

No homeless on the streets—
                  A sadness
Felt by the bare pavement
              At dawn.

                  Patrick T. Randolph
                  La Crosse, Wisconsin

Origin of Homelessness

Has there ever been
                    a more homeless man
                                        than God?

                              Patrick T. Randolph
                              La Crosse, Wisconsin

The Cold Truth

A homeless man
  was found draped over the steps
    at the entrance of the DuPont Starbucks
      on Connecticut Avenue
        yesterday morning.

He tried
to wait out January's biting night
but set solid, curled, fetus-like, on the trendy
    steps—
one Frozen Mocha Frappuccino,
low fat, decaf, dead.

No one noticed
he had crossed over—too busy—
until the pale morning sun thawed the crystallized
    cells
        and the body slumped sideways
        like excess foam dribbled over life's rim.

The regulars complained—
latte access is blocked!
The manager summoned the police, who
slid the triangular-shaped body like a maple scone
into a man-sized brown paper envelope.

The officers were rewarded with
one free pastry each.
"Thanks," mumbled the venti-blond policewoman
through a bite of sour-cream coffee cake.
      Crumbs tumbled from her mouth.

Empty Shoes

The hardscrabble coins
   from the dead beggar's cup
      were tossed clinking to the barista's tip jar.
         Their echo rattled down the now-empty steps
         and dissipated into the brittle frozen air.

Jackson Lassiter
Washington, DC

Abandoned Laundromat

Murphy's Laundromat closed down months ago,
Paper sign in the window says "LEASE NOW!"
Rancid water puddles stand on the floor,
Reflecting neon lights from Bob's Sports Bar.

Every night Al passes the laundromat,
He peers inside, still sees her sitting there
Next to the vending machine, with tired eyes—
She'd rock in the chair like a confused child.

It always seemed she had no place to go,
But she never bothered the customers—
Truth is, they bothered her; she'd turn away
And pretend to read meaning in her hands.

Now with Murphy's Laundromat boarded up,
Al wonders where that girl's gone to stay sane.
Where does she go to stay out of the cold?
Why, he wonders, he never asked her name.

She appeared wild—an untamed alley cat,
A free spirit—any man's wild lover,
And yet her eyes seemed like those of a sage—
A wise, ancient, sophisticated soul.

Her hair was always well kept—long and brown.
Occasionally she'd use red lipstick
And eye shadow to cover dark secrets,
Her skin pale white—a pure, cold-winter Moon.

Her clothes were common, but she had good taste,
She'd wear light blue pants and a dark blue blouse,
Her worn jean jacket was clean and smelled good;
She'd use a strange perfume—mystically sweet.

153

Empty Shoes

It was odd, she pretended to wash clothes—
She'd get up every hour or so and check
The machines, examining her ghost garments,
Then sit down and stare at her worn, tired hands.

Al's reflection now looks back at himself,
He finds his face smiling with thoughts of her—
And hopes that tonight she has found a home
Where she can dream with eyes closed in deep
    sleep.

                        Patrick T. Randolph
                        La Crosse, Wisconsin

Exposed

"Monster"—

That's what a well-dressed little girl called me
yesterday on the street. I didn't know
at first how to take it. I once was a lover

of monsters; watched Creature Double Feature
every Saturday, back when I was a boy—
zombie Nazis and golden gargoyles,

giant mummies and vampire surfers, back-to-
back, all of them dancing in black and white.
I learned to look closely, and before the end

invariably spied a zipper on the spine,
a missing contact—one eye red, one brown—
unpainted flesh on Frankenstein's waistband,

some telltale sign of the person underneath,
working an unforgiving gig, playing
a part in a world where creatures never lasted.

My seams should be easier to spot than those
of a costume. I can feel the cold through them,
almost as sharp as a cruel word.

Noel Sloboda
York, Pennsylvania

ೞ **V** ೲ

Suffer, die, or get well; but, above all, live until your last hour.

Jean-Jacques Rousseau:
Emile *or* On Education

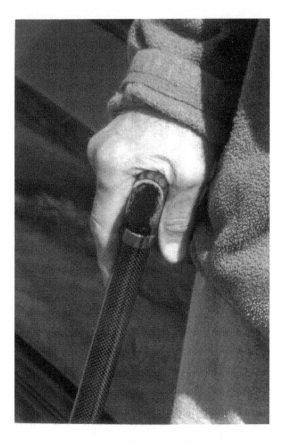

Pondering the Sun

Stranger

One of those ordinary mornings:
she cradled her burden, bowed
down like a tree bulging with conkers.

The station heaved with arrivals:
backpackers passed by, jostling,
teeming like termites. Her feet

struck matches on ice-edged
cobbles. She carried on walking,
stumbling, drifting. The smart

of chestnut smoke unfettered
floodgates of exile. Her tears
froze, frosting the pigeons.

One of those ordinary evenings:
the first ripe conker fell.
She set light to her burden,

firewood for the hearth of "home."

Caroline Gill
Swansea, Wales, UK

Impossible Habitat

In innocence
    i built my home
    of toothpicks
    bright steel washers
    & passing pink clouds,

lived comfortably therein
    until one day
    a front-page story
    declared my home
    impossible—

& now i live
    exposed
    to the elements—
ashamed
    in my nakedness.

Spiel
Pueblo West, Colorado

Pane

Big City Uptown Lady

"Happy, Happy Birthday,
Dear Victoria!"

She stands at her corner
in all makes of weather—
leather shoes,
a fuzzy hat as brown
as her eyes.
She holds out a blue and white
"I Love New York" coffee cup
for small change.
"It's for the shelter,"
she says,
"where I stay."

Morning office drones,
dawdling midday tourists,
and evening swanks
throw coins to ease
overworked guilt.
Job and home
are the only fences between
them and her.

On this October day
amid dimes and quarters,
one golden peep-show token,
and a candy bar
with chocolate sweet as love,
she sits in a warm bed
of cold pavement
singing,

"Happy, Happy Birthday,
Dear Victoria—
Dear Me, Dear You.
Could you spare
another dime?"

Mary Jo Stich
Denmark, Wisconsin

Istanbul:
Song of a Homeless Man

A heart has stopped beating tonight in the city
By the sea. Soon they'll find his silenced body,
Pronounce him dead, prepare a grave. Few
    mourners
Will come—one might weep, reflect, let memories
Soak his soul like May rain. No one can take his
    place
In this city, the unfortunate will never make his
Acquaintance, never meet his eyes, hear his stories.
When his heart stopped, a part of humanity
Vanished, a part of this town faded, a fragment of
    God
Disappeared, leaving this small world empty
Of a voice that could soothe you like a dream.

Patrick T. Randolph
La Crosse, Wisconsin

Istanbul at Dawn

Dead seagull—feathers
Flutter in the morning breeze.
Homeless woman's eyes

Look down on silent white death,
Giving her passion to live.

Patrick T. Randolph
La Crosse, Wisconsin

Where Angels Walk

At Graveside

Of burials without coffins we heard many instances…
they tell a fearful story.

William E. Forster, 1847

At the mound where you lie
swaddled in the blight
that bedded you, abducted you
from your grim pallet,
the mourners come to kneel,
their hearts ravaged
as though plucked by crows.

Hear them, lost one,
though lowered now
to the press of chilled earth fingers,
the erasure of hunger-marked flesh;
they beg eternity's balm
for your unhoused bones.

With lingerers' prayers
they encase you in remembrance;
with lingerers' tears
they nail their love around you
and kiss the lid.

Jeri McCormick
Madison, Wisconsin

Winter Classroom

Homeless man
Laughs in the rain—

Memory of third grade—
Gold star placed on his spelling quiz,

Reflecting the florescent lights in the warm Winter
    classroom.

Patrick T. Randolph
La Crosse, Wisconsin

Diary of a Homeless Soul

All class period Mr. Hart noticed the dead wasp
On the floor in front of the chalkboard.
He tried not to step on it, feeling somehow
It would pick itself up and fly out the door.

Barb was in elementary school watching him teach,
She tries now, like he did, not to step on the
    wasp—
Trying not to step on this life of hers, hoping
It will pick itself up and fly out the door.

Patrick T. Randolph
La Crosse, Wisconsin

To Have, to Give, to Receive

Gnarled and Stooped

Like the gnarled and stooped
witch-hazel tree,
fragrant blossoms spent,
their bent forms lean over
that of their daughter's,
now ruined and wasted.
As wind rushing through limbs
whose tensility lack the strength
to bear this blow,
their arms hang in desolate,
despairing bewilderment.
The ticking passage of precious time,
like a bell's knell,
pounds nails one by one into
their fertile hopes,
sealing into grim, black reality
that bitter fate—eternal loss.
Tears splash disbelief as it
pommels the sickroom walls
with silent shrieks begging an answer!
Why had not the gift
that meant life
come one sunrise sooner?

Thea F. Daigler
Tucson, Arizona

Shame and Shiny Shoes
in New Delhi

With a comforting snap
   of the purse,
      I contain the grownup
         until I reach the car.
      Opening the door
         with the importance of
            errand completion,
      I slam away maturity
         and recall the snappy click
            of my Mary Janes[16]—
               they, one month new;
               me, four years old.
         The black shiny shoes
            with a silver-tongued buckle
            kept my wild toes
               in a tidy package.
And, in these Mary Janes,
   I sang "Mary Had a Little Lamb"
into a tape recorder
   in the Tape Recorder Store in the
      middle of hot, limp New Delhi—
   my audience:
      my musically discerning father,
         the shopkeeper,
      and a silent woman in the doorway,
         begging in a ragged sari,
            toes unfettered,
         dust delicate on powdered soles,

---

[16] Mary Janes are strap shoes or sandals for women.
Traditionally they were worn predominantly by young
girls.

170

a murky shadow of a life,
   the listless veil of hunger
      hanging over her inscrutable presence.
I looked down at my Mary Janes
   and up at hunger—
   finished my song.
My reedy Australian voice played back,
   mocking, it seemed,
     my ragged sari audience,
and I felt ashamed at four
   of having anything
     shiny and black,
       which were not—
                eyes.

Katrin Talbot
Madison, Wisconsin

Feed Them

Then he said to them, "You give them something to eat."
                                                    Mark 6:37

Give them grandma's buttermilk biscuits. Give them
your favorite comfort food. Give them your
homemade yogurt and, too, the cup of milk left
        on the
counter all weekend long. Give them the aromatic
soup. Give them the soup kitchen, pungent with what
everyone brings, with what everyone leaves at home.
Give whatever it takes to feed them.

Put something fresh in their hands, their mouths, up
their noses. Put something raw in their ears. Put
something well aged in their cups, well cooked in
        their
bowls, well trained in their paths. Put something sticky
in their pockets. Lay something extraordinarily rare at
their feet—at toe or heel, whatever they allow—and
pray it feeds them.

Give them the farm and the village, the cow and the
inn. Give them silver, the time of day and a detailed
set of directions. Give them your mom who knew
how to choose a good caterer. Give them your dad
who was always the better cook. Give them your
baby's milk breath, and baby's milk diaper. Milk your
roots for all they're worth. Then feed them.

Give them the bald unexplainable fact. Give them the
semantically productive metaphor with no scientific
basis. Give them the dubiousness of your doubt. Give

them the nut and the cracker. Give them
    something to
break their teeth and sooth their throats. Give
everything you know and everything you don't. By all
means, feed them.

Yes, even the blood in your veins, without conditions,
nutritional information, or suggestions for serving.
Hand it over in your best luggage, wearing your good
suit. Give it with a new garbage pail and a Hefty liner
for what doesn't keep; give it with an airsick bag for
what doesn't fly. Give it already in the kitchen sink. So
long as you feed them.

Give them the foretaste and the aftertaste. Give them
the rocks, the dust, the lean mean light. Give them the
pretense, the intense, and the tent posts. Give
    them the
40 acres and the 40 years. Give the whole damn lonely,
especially if it's the only place you have to hand. And
don't forget the odd bit of toast in the other hand;
that, or the sardines and the last half bottle of
homemade wine. Just feed them.

                    Shelly L. Hall
                    Waukesha, Wisconsin

Fire-Soaked Forest

Following the Star, 1847

We get by on gleanings from the shore
at Killybegs[17]—cockles, fluke fish,
slouk weed, dúlamán[18] and turnips
from the neighbors, who merit sainthood.
We lost our women to the bloody flux,
and the rest of the kin to Canada.

Unable to pay the rent, we three—grandfather,
father, and son—stay on at the mercy of Mr.
    Wright,
the landlord, whose patience began to rot
along with the potatoes back in September.
The knock comes on a raw March day,
confirming eviction. We pack what little

we own and join the onlookers—police, bailiff,
neighbors, and the landlord himself, who
preaches highhandedly to the group, offering
the prize of a full pound to anyone who will
start the fire. Colum, that devious son of mine,
up and grabs the spade, reenters the cabin,

struts out with a hunk of smoldering turf
from the hearth. We stand, a solemn
congregation, as he tosses it neatly
onto the roof thatch. The Holy Spirit hovers
as wind and blaze perform their work; the Kellys
make the sign of the cross, and Mr. Wright

---

[17] Killybegs is considered Ireland's premier fishing port.
It is located on the northwest coast of Ireland in
County Donegal.
[18] *Dúlamán* means *seaweed* in Irish Gaelic.

stiffens like a snuffed-out candle. Colum crooks
his grin, extends a palm, pockets the coin; old Da[19]
positions his cane; I shoulder my pride, lift the sack
that holds our earthly goods. We bow absolution
to the ashen-faced one, wave to the crowd,
and like the three kings of old, consult the sky.

Jeri McCormick
Madison, Wisconsin

---

[19] *Da* is a colloquial Irish term meaning Dad, Pa or
Papa.

Fat Eddy

I had a good friend,
Fat Eddy was his name.
He liked to smoke pot
And sniff a little cocaine.

Truly, a godly and pious man,
A reader of the Bible,
He knew the Lord would understand
Then forgive his pursuits, mostly idle.

Fat Eddy was a wonderer,
A mover and a shaker,
Born to Gypsy parents
With the heart of a Quaker.

Fat Eddy wouldn't choose
Between the Lady and the Creator—
One day he went the way of all Gypsy souls
To snort coke with the Maker.

Dave Dolle
La Crosse, Wisconsin

Stutter Step

Today I wake up with a headache.

I look around and find
fragments of my life
everywhere
except where
I thought I'd been.

Every step I take
my heart spins and shakes.

Every time I look
through the time of dread,
all I see
is a life without reason,
a life out of rhyme.

Fragments of sleep still haunt me
when I look to the West.
In this life's twilight I stutter.
I step. I stutter.

Stutter.
Where…where shall I step?
Stutter.
Where…where shall I rest?

David Hart
La Crosse, Wisconsin

Nothing

A good fart
Deserves a few eager ears
And a couple devil-may-care grins!

Nothing—not even a fart—
Should be left homeless
In this world of our whimsical sins!

Patrick T. Randolph
La Crosse, Wisconsin

Homeless Minstrel

Old man farted on a crosstown bus,
Don't know why the world made such a fuss,
Sure his music smelled bad,
Made you want to go mad,
But each toot had such a rhythmic cuss!

Patrick T. Randolph
La Crosse, Wisconsin

There but for the Grace of God...

A stumble and a limp.
Enough that the neighborhood kids called him
     monster.
Dirty clothes and downcast eyes.
Worn-out shoes, filthy hands, hair matted and
     beard gone wild.
Everyone knew to move away
When he walked towards them as the sun went down.
No one ever spoke to him
Out of ignorance and foolish mortal fear.

Behind the laundromat
He slept under an open vent and by a boarded-up
     door.
Someone had seen him there—
Wrapped in just his arms and a damp newspaper.
Eyes filled with clear malice.
No one wanted to get too close and take a risk.

Everyone thought that he was right out of prison,
Or maybe released from a place far darker and far
     worse.
Yes, he was crazier than a loon—
Let out to mingle with the public just a bit too early.

But no one knew the truth—
He was damaged while on his job of twenty years—
Health, job, family now gone.
No one left to help him stand on his own two feet.

Empty Shoes

We never took the time
To consider that he didn't have a chance at all,
That he was a victim
Deserving of our help and concern.

Simple stories never are—
And our judgments simply hide the mystery we
    can't understand.

Andy Davis
Houston, Minnesota

Midnight Winter Hug

In homeless castle,
Two gained an intimate warmth
By linking a deep

Pompei-fed embrace that spilled
Heartfelt lava-like love—everywhere!

Gerald R. Randolph
Rice Lake, Wisconsin

Embrace

Homelessness: A Prison Break

One more day to breathe,
Let's make a pact with robins—
They sing their way through.

Why not copy these creatures?
Make it a Spring holiday.

Gerald R. Randolph
Rice Lake, Wisconsin

I Keep My Eyes Straight Ahead

As I enter the parking lot at my grocery store, a
    hulking disheveled man on the
corner holds a small white sign:
    "Home
     Less"
I look away and drive on. "Don't stare!" Mother
    used to say.

I buy risotto with fresh chanterelle mushrooms.
    Meet my girlfriends at The Café
for lunch. We kiss, share news, clink our glasses of
    crisp chardonnay. There
he is again as I leave: long brown hair and beard,
    shirts with holes, dirty pants
and sneakers. I keep my eyes straight ahead.

The next week I put aside two dollars in the cup
    holder. After a salad of baby
greens, artichoke hearts, and feta cheese, I drive
    beside him, lower the window
and hand him the money. He takes it, smiles, says,
    "God Bless You."
I drive away fast.

The next week my friends say, "The homeless just
    buy alcohol." I order a cheeseburger and large
    coffee to go. My girlfriends' eyebrows arch.
    When I hand the bag to him,
he pulls it into his chest, and runs away—up the
    slope behind bushes.

I notice how much he mumbles. I give him two
    dollars each week and get his huge smile and a
    "God Bless You," which seems to lighten my
    breathing.

Black garbage bags crowd the bushes. I say to the
    clerk, "…a homeless man
on the corner." "I'll tell the manager you
    complained," she responds. "Oh, no, I was
    thinking, a shelter…a church…."

After our salads that day, I give him five dollars,
    less, I realize, than I tip the waiter.
I see homeless people under the overpass. Were
    they there before?

That week three big teenage boys on bikes
    surround him. His arms flop.
He drops his sign. How dare they hassle "my"
    homeless man! I look away.

The next week he is gone. I am glad.

Henrietta Sparks
Carpinteria, California

187

Snow Songs at Noon

I Don't Know

I don't know any homeless,
But I know all about them.

Don't talk to me
About plants closing down,
Or living paycheck to paycheck—
Two weeks away from nowhere to go.
They've got boots and straps
To pull themselves up with—
Hard work is all it takes.

I don't know any homeless,
But I know all about them.

Don't lecture me
About closed-up hospitals,
Or the sick wandering the streets
With no one to take care of them.
There are prisons and the like;
Let them sleep there—
It's the price they pay.

I don't know any homeless,
But I know all about them.

Don't cry to me
About their addictions,
Or being lost in a hazy world
Created by personal weakness.
It's a simple matter of self-control—
No one makes them do those things.
They just have to say "No."

189

Empty Shoes

I don't know any homeless,
But I know all about them.

Don't talk to me
About how fortunate I am—
I've worked hard for everything I have,
I take care of me and mine.
I don't have time for anyone else.
No compassion and no caring.
I've got my own life to live.

I don't know any homeless,
But I know all about them.

Andy Davis
Houston, Minnesota

Anonymous

I

Neither here nor there
nor anywhere.

A solitary soul
that never grows old.

A detached heart
from the very start

of every occasion
of every persuasion

when life on the street
just can't be beat.

A detached, solitary,
reminiscent soul.

Neither here nor there
nor anywhere.

II

Neither care nor dare
can set things straight.

Neither fate nor destiny,
nor public isolation.
And standing upright
doesn't make man bright.

Empty Shoes

Empty phrases strike deep
while throats mumble and weep.

Hear my friends now:
"I don't see color"—
"Just *look* at them."

But sitting here on my thumbs
doesn't make me right.

III

A solitary soul
quarrels with itself.

"Walk softly and carry
a big philosophy," and

"Better you than me," it says,
treading lightly.

A detached heart
from the very start—

Neither here nor there
nor anywhere.

David Hart
La Crosse, Wisconsin

Edge of Night

Black with blue swollen veins
he sits in stained denim
on the train-station bench

elbows on spread-eagle knees
sparrow hands on head hung low
a plastic produce bag for a hat

pulled over his ears
preserving the rising heat
protecting the fragile lobes from frostbite

as winter eats its way
into the San Francisco Bay
with butcher knife teeth

Ellaraine Lockie
Sunnyvale, California

Sometimes God Sends Messages

to Sam The Man: the drip in a drainpipe,
the stare of a seagull, an old man exploring
his ear with a pen, the music pulsing
from a trembling car, and the light,
in every f-stop and shutter speed,
from the gray of a Seattle morning
to the visual caterwauling
when the sun barges in.

A Goddess in a yellow dress
approaches, Her body moving
like birthday balloons.

A definite signal.

Sam usually notices when God speaks
but often isn't sure what He's saying. Probably
the usual: *I am who I am. Don't worry; be happy.*
Love your neighbor. Stay off the crack.
God talks to Sam like he's a moron,
but Sam doesn't mind, figuring he's more
than earned God's skepticism.

This morning, each person on First Avenue
is a syllable in God's monologue, a note
in His song, until Sam gets into the rhythm
and slaps out a beat on his thighs as he walks,
noticing the various incarnations passing by:

a woman—a man—a man,
a woman—a man,
a man—man—man,

—woman.

Roger Midgett
Bainbridge Island, Washington

194

Sam the Man Dispenses

tears from a mechanism of pain,
chronic yet intermittent, grinding
directly behind his eyes,
as he sits on a bench in Occidental Park,
recalling the first blow: a sucker punch
delivered on the playground by a kid
named Aloysius, brief whistle in his ear,
rapid shift in vision to the right,
jarring Sam beyond the piles of dirty snow
and the brick of St. Theresa's parochial school
into a river flowing deep beneath the earth.

That first was followed by thumps
in alleys, bars, and logging camps,
in factory restrooms, fields,
ditches, and holding cells,
delivered by fists and two-by-fours,
Louisville Sluggers, rebar, jack handles,
and even, going back to when
Sam was nineteen, a Christmas tree,
lights and all, that cousin Ray,
drunk on schnapps and enraged
by a lack of presents,
swung like a battle-axe,
exploding ornaments on the walls,
catching Sam with the foot
of the metal tree stand
clean in his temple
where he still bears a slot
deep enough to hold a dime.

Roger Midgett
Bainbridge Island, Washington

William

William comes to my office asking for help.
Despite the clean shirt and jeans, he looks as if
he's just escaped from the bone wagon.[20]

Are you on the cocktail?[21] I ask.
No, he says, *when I take it with methadone I get really sick.*

William drives me to check out his new apartment
in a new Saturn, borrowed, I hope.
He's extremely polite, soft-spoken. I'm beginning
to like him more than I should.
He pulls up to a gas station, gets out, and tells
the attendant to fill it with Super.

Then he pops his head into the car and says:

> *When I was eight, my mother left me on a street*
> *corner, told me to wait. She never came back.*
> *I hung around until a black lady took me home*
> *and raised me with her own. Skinny Latino kid*
> *in the projects, I got beat up every day.*

This is more than I need to know. The deal's been
struck.

---

[20] A *bone wagon* was used to carry dead bodies of the poor
to the graveyard or the "boneyard" to be buried in
paupers' graves. Sometimes, in order to free up a hospital
bed, a poor individual who was not yet dead would be
tossed outside to be carted away by a bone wagon.
[21] *Cocktail* here refers to a treatment regimen that
usually includes a combination of several drugs, so that
their combined effect is more powerful than any of the
drugs used individually.

Back on the road, he says:

> *To stay alive, I sold drugs, heroin mostly. I was good*
> *at it, made lots of money, didn't use. Curiosity finally*
> *did me in. With my T-cell count, I should be dead.*

We've breached the line, so I ask, *Are they okay?*

They're both free, he says. *Jessica wanted a baby. It's a miracle,*
don't you think?

I don't say what I think: *Get off the damn methadone, get*
    on meds.
You made a son, now be a father.

The apartment is in a clean building. We move from
    room to room.
I test light switches, flush the toilet, turn on the hot
    water.
William trails me, a hapless lamb, *Thank you. Thank*
    you, he says.
No swagger, not the brash dealer who did a stretch.

I find an excuse to call him every month.

His wife runs off with another man, gives him the child.
He can't get off the methadone, buys his son a puppy,
sends me a photo of William, Jr. on his second
    birthday—
chubby, wide-eyed, and smiling.

Nancy Scott
Lawrenceville, New Jersey

Eighteenth Birthday

Antoine learned how to be that extra child
in someone else's house,
wear hand-me-downs and skip meals,
the kid with the different last name.
If he made too much noise,
got in trouble at school,
or the foster payment came late,
his belongings got packed in a brown paper bag.
If a government car brought a stranger to ask,
How're you doing? bullshit like that,
his heart went ballistic, his mouth kept silent.

One ordinary day, he heard words
like the slash of a box cutter,
Your dad's in jail; your mom's been sober;
we're taking you home.
This skinny twelve-year-old bolted,
ran barefoot down broken cement, shouted,
I'd rather be dead than go back there.

The day he turned eighteen
Antoine was put out of the shelter.
Baggy jeans,
immaculate Nikes,
hair twisted in dreads,
a stuffed backpack slung over his shoulder,
he stood at the curb with no place to go,
bouncing his head to a Walkman's beat.

Nancy Scott
Lawrenceville, New Jersey

What They Dream about
at the Shelter

Mostly about heat. Enameled stoves
appear in some, their open
oven doors rolling out warmth
so real that the dreamers wake up

astonished at the morning chill
and their thin socks. At breakfast,
holding tight to coffee cups,
they silently hoard dreams of

furnaces powerful as kings,
and bathroom mirrors
opaque with steam as water
rushes from a tap. Other dreams

are harder to describe—
dreams just of dreaming under
clean sheets and blankets,
dreams of doors with locks.

Dori Appel
Ashland, Oregon

Woman Without a Home

Who could have known
that poetry would have to face
your eyes on every corner and turn away
bereft of words again, offering to
your cracked hand only pennies
for safe passage across the rushing street
to the Land of the Lost. And one day
you are gone.

The hole you left in the air cries out
like the mouth of whatever you once were,
whatever you saw and felt before the grave.

I am elected to speak of you,
though, I too, often go begging
in my safe apartment with no one
to talk to, no place to rest my head.

Bill Zavatsky
New York City, New York

L.A. River

Clouds slice a mountain
in half, making snow
covered peaks appear
to float separately
above.

Rain stained aqueduct—
slimy green shimmers
wink in the sunlight.

Ralph ascends the
fence; a sign reads
"No Dumping."
He climbs over
the concrete wall
of this faux river.

Ralph slips on damp
slime, skids to
the center, flops
on his butt.

A plastic trash bag
bursts beneath
him, spews empty
cans and bottles
outward:
A *recycle garden*
of plastic bottles and
aluminum cans now
in full bloom.
He stands,
reclaims his booty,
unzips his fly,
and urinates.

Empty Shoes

Yellow splash
on green slime.
Blue tributary
heads straight
to the ocean.

Vehicles pass
overhead—
Ralph sits in
the shade beneath
Grand Avenue.
A school bus whizzes by—
raucous kids don't notice
him below.

He walks east
by south, follows
the meager trickle.
A striped cat yawns,
ignores his greeting,
licks her belly fur.

Wall Street Journal
pages carpet the
ground:
"Oil Prices Up,"
"Dow Jones Falls,"
"Average Rents Rise,"
"Health Benefits Cut."
Ralph saves some
pages to invest
in his future—
The ocean front
could be chilly tonight.

Thomas L. Conroy
San Clemente, California

Mother & Child

Wheels & tracks, Baby,
Don't worry, I ain't gonna
Let you be taken. Hush-a-bye.
Hush-a-bye. Sleep now, that's right.
I got a couple hundred dollars.
In this knapsack, you're pretty
Much hid, just in case. You know
That welfare lady's put out some
Warrant? O.K.
We're hitching a ride & will hop
The next train soon. 3 A.M.—
I think it's early enough,
The whole station is still groggy.
Thank God, it's rainin', good
Warm muggy dust of diesel…
Makes me wanna doze too.
Come on, Hon, don't wake up.
Here's your old tick tock clock,
Just like a heart, & I'm right
With ya, rockin' soft & close.
"La la la." You see, I have to
Sing quiet, 'cause they're takin'
Our ticket & hey, lettin' us board.
Nobody suspects. Want your bottle?
Look at those lights, the whole
City a Christmas tree blinkin'
"So long" as we plunge—
Express cargo—into the
Clickety-clack, clickety-clack
Of this safe moving dark.

Stephen Mead
Albany, New York

X-Ray Glasses

People's secrets
leap at me
like fleas off the sidewalk.

Desperate eyes home in on mine.
Drunks drone on about wasted years and pain.

Do I have a disease?
Silent sonar signaling that
of all the people on the bus,
I should be the one to tell their stories to?

With x-ray glasses that won't come off,
I see the reasons for the furrowed brow,
    the clutched fist,
    the bitten nails.

Sometimes, like a ministering angel,
I want to sweep them up, smooth their brows
and tell them it'll be okay.

But sometimes I don't believe myself.
I want to shut them out,
take off the damn glasses
and go home.

Later, at the computer,
words come pouring through my fingertips,
speaking for friends and lovers
and the strangers on the bus,
speaking for people
with no words of their own.
Only thoughts and feelings
longing to be heard.

Shizue Seigel
San Francisco, California

Oyster Girl

I began to walk to the desks clustered in a circle;
book read, homework done, thoughts in place,
but you shepherded me to the shell in the corner
and bade me to crawl in
lest the homeless girl
contaminate the other more desirable students in
     the class.

And for awhile
my newfound classroom abode
seemed to do quite nicely;
the loneliness was exquisite
and the jade color of the interior,
not unlike frost-covered evergreens,
was almost soothing.

But for some reason
you kept throwing angry words my way—
words that irritated like grains of sand,
words that caused my epithelial cells
to begin to secrete.

So I cannot help but wonder
how you will react
when in June, 2009,
the shell is finally opened
and it is revealed
that I am the pearl of the class.

Amelia Levchenko
Wheeling, Illinois

Lamplight

After the Poetry Reading

My friend and I came out
into a warm night of moonlight.
The sand glistened. We walked
toward the ocean;
silver paths led to the horizon.

Light and free,
we carried our sandals,
curled our toes in sand,
drifted toward the lap of waves.

Suddenly, a huge shaggy man
lurched from below a dune, shirts flapping,
his face hidden by a beard.
Around him, moonlight reflected on the sand.

Startled, we stopped; my friend grabbed my hand.
The man gestured as if to say, "Come here."
Arms spread wide, his hands embraced the shore,
a conductor calling his orchestra.

I moved toward him; my friend pulled back.
He nodded to me, turned and sat down—
his face toward the sea, head upthrust, bathing in
    the sky.
We, too, filled our faces with moonlight.

He hummed and inquired, "You poets?"

I said a quick, "Yes."
He continued, "I came up for food and heard.
    Made me wanna sing."

I felt like singing, too. Yet we sat in silence.
He shivered. I asked, "Are you cold?"
"Yeah."

In the distance a sleeping-bag cocoon nestled in a
    hollow.
"Why don't you go to the shelter?" I suggested.
"Never can live in walls again, feels like death," he
    said.

Moonlight traced his weathered face, his bearing a
    military man's.
"Were you in Vietnam?"
He nodded.

Again we sat in silence; he shivered and looked up
at the stars.

Henrietta Sparks
Carpinteria, California

Where They Once Sat

Park in January

No flowers in bloom, Winter trees
Speak in inward silence.

Snowflakes keep their mouths closed—
Concentrating on flight.

Words tossed around by a homeless
Man on a metal bench

Are consumed cravingly
By the Wind.

Patrick T. Randolph
La Crosse, Wisconsin

Why Hurry?

It's pouring today.
In the car, waiting for the light to turn green,
I see a woman crossing the street,
pushing her possession-filled cart.
Trusting her homemade plastic poncho to keep
    her dry,
she looks down to keep raindrops
from getting in her eyes.

When she raises her head to see the light,
I recognize her face and recall all the places I've
    seen her before:
at the library, on Sundays, listening to football
    games on her
handheld radio, but never reading books;
standing in front of the bank,
but never going inside;
waiting at bus stops,
but never boarding for a ride.

She now tries hard to get to someplace
on this rain-soaked day.
Where is she going?
Why doesn't she hide and wait for the rain to stop
since she has no one to meet,
no errands to run,
nowhere to go?
And yet, at the same time,
I realize, she can do what she pleases.
She belongs everywhere—
the whole world is hers.

Gamze Randolph
La Crosse, Wisconsin

Empty Shoes

Contributors

Greta Aart lives in Paris, France. Besides writing, she also plays classical piano and the ancient Chinese zither. Aart hopes to continue to bring music and poetry to the homeless.

M. Lee Alexander's poetry has appeared in numerous journals, and her chapbook *Observatory* was published in 2007. She teaches creative writing at William and Mary and resides in Williamsburg, Virginia.

Austin Alexis has contributed to canned-food drives for homeless at New York City College of Technology. He has written fiction about homelessness and was a Bronx Arts Council panelist.

Dori Appel has been a Red Cross disaster volunteer for several years. She is the author of a collection of poems, *Another Rude Awakening*, as well as many produced and published plays.

Linda Aschbrenner of Marshfield, Wisconsin, published the poetry journal *Free Verse*, issues one through 100. In addition, her Marsh River Editions has published 16 chapbooks. She works with homeless poems.

Mary Jo Balistreri lives each day with her husband in a poem of woods, water, and wild life. Besides writing, she enjoys reading, gardening, and playing the piano. She is also involved with the local food pantry and has worked with Loaves and Fishes. Her book of poems, *Joy in the Morning*, was published in 2008.

Madeleine Beckman is the author of *Dead Boyfriends*, a poetry collection (LinearArts Books). Ms. Beckman works as an editor and teaches creative writing and journalism at Stern College for Women. She lives in New York City.

Scott J. Brooks was born and raised in rural Sheboygan, Wisconsin, on the western shores of Lake Michigan. He is currently a counselor in Oshkosh, where he works with people with disabilities.

Alan Catlin recently retired from his unchosen profession as a barman to concentrate on his poetry and his fictional memoirs. Catlin's latest poetry chapbooks are *Only the Dead Know Albany*, from sunnyoutside.com, *The Effects of Sunlight on Fog*, from Bright Hill, and *Me in Suits*, from Madman Ink.

Jan Chronister lives in Maple, Wisconsin, and teaches writing part time. Fresh produce from her garden goes to the Union Gospel Mission in Duluth, Minnesota, whenever possible.

Tom L. Conroy is a poet and a publisher/editor of *The League of Laboring Poets*. He volunteers at an abused women's safe haven, where he teaches them how to keep journals and start to express themselves through their writing.

Thea F. Daigler taught high school for 25 years. After the passing of her 15-year-old son, she took to writing to calm the homelessness of her psyche. Daigler lives in Tucson, Arizona.

Andrew Davis was in Illinois, moved around a lot, and ended up in Houston, Minnesota. Davis has a job, but writing fiction, drama, essays, and the occasional poem constitute his true desire.

Krikor Der Hohannesian's work has appeared in numerous literary journals, including *The Evansville Review*, *The South Carolina Review*, *Atlanta Review*, *The New Renaissance*, and *Permafrost*. He also serves as Assistant Treasurer of the New England Poetry Club.

Bruce Dethlefsen delivered telegrams, was a night watchman in a cave, taught juggling, and set up libraries in Honduras. Bruce has three poetry volumes published and lives in Westfield, Wisconsin.

Dave Dolle lives in La Crosse, Wisconsin. He works as a physical therapist technician at Franciscan-Skemp Hospital. He is thoroughly in love with writing and practicing the Japanese martial art of Aikido. Dolle is currently working on his second novel.

Mary L. Downs volunteered at LEAVEN, an assistance program for people in crisis. Her poems have appeared in *Fox Cry Review*, *The Lyric*, and the *Wisconsin Poets' Calendar*.

Naomi Fast earned her M.A. in Creative Writing from Portland State University, where she was the recipient of an Academy of American Poets Award. The Willamette and Congo rivers often appear in her poetry.

Barbara Flaherty, author of *Holy Madness*, dedicated to her brother who died on the streets, and *Doing It Another Way: The Basic Text*, has volunteered in two shelters and supervised a treatment center for homeless people.

Gretchen Fletcher leads writing workshops for Florida Center for the Book, in Ft. Lauderdale. Her poems have appeared in anthologies and journals including *The Formalist*, *Inkwell*, and *Poetry as Spiritual Practice*.

Nancy Gauquier has once been homeless and stayed in a shelter in New York. Currently, she lives in Santa Cruz, California. Her poems have appeared in *Free Verse*, *Poesy*, *Blind Man's Rainbow*, *Zen Baby*, *Thema*, and online in *Flashquake* and *Andwerve*.

Caroline Gill, winner of the 2007 Petra Kenney Poetry Competition (general section), lives in Swansea, Wales, UK. She has worked alongside international refugees in Rome as a mission Field Partner.

Ed Galing, at 90 years of age, has been termed "Poet of the Greatest Generation." He is a World War II veteran and former columnist. Galing is the poet laureate of Hatboro, Pennsylvania. He has been published in *Main Street Rag*, *HazMat Review,* and many other journals in the States.

Kenneth P. Gurney, author of *A Place to Keep Spent Time* and *Greeting Card and Other Poems*, lives in Albuquerque, New Mexico, where he manages a stress-free existence with the wind.

Shelly L. Hall lives and writes in Waukesha, Wisconsin. She is the author of two volumes of poetry: *Tonguebones* and *Mind of Cups*.

David Hart teaches English at the University of Wisconsin-La Crosse. He fills notebooks with poetry, short stories, and folk-music lyrics, when he is not biking or playing guitar.

Deborah Hauser is a poet, writer, and teacher living in Babylon, New York, with her husband and her two cats, Hunter and Hemingway. She has published poetry in *Focus: Stony Brook University Women's Studies Department Literary Journal, Midwest Poetry Review,* and *Sotto Voce*.

Laura Heidy-Halberstein lives in Alexandria, Virginia, and is a former medic who worked a simultaneous 12 years in an Indiana ER and for the Munster Fire Department.

Randall Horton is an advocate for the homeless and for prison reform, having been homeless and in prison. Currently, he teaches at SUNY Albany and is a Ph.D. candidate in Creative Writing.

Susan Kileen writes from her century-old farmhouse and is a member of Stone Kettle Poets. Her work has appeared in *Wisconsin Review,* the *Wisconsin Poets' Calendar, Free Verse, Rock River Anthology,* and *Poetry and Praise.* She is a recipient of the Wisconsin Regional Writers' Association Jade Ring Award for short stories.

Judy Kolosso obsesses over saving wild places and Wisconsin barns. She writes from her home near Slinger and from her family's farm in Neenah.

217

Ellen Kort served as Wisconsin's first poet laureate from 2000 to 2004. She has received several state and national awards and travels widely as a speaker and workshop facilitator.

Jackson Lassiter is the Administrative Director for the George Washington University School of Business, Department of Tourism and Hospitality Management. His poems have appeared online in *Glass: A Journal of Poetry*, *Boiling River*, and *Umbrella Poetry Journal*, and in print in *Apocalypse Literary Arts Magazine*.

Janet Leahy is an advocate for peace and justice. Her chapbook is titled *The Storm, Poems of War, Iraq*. She lives and writes in New Berlin, Wisconsin.

Michele Leavitt experienced homelessness as a teenage runaway in the 1970s. During the 1980s and 1990s, she represented homeless people as a public defender and also worked for a shelter for battered women. Some of her family members are currently homeless.

Sharmagne Leland-St. John, a 2007 Pushcart Prize nominee, is a Native American poet, a concert performer, a lyricist, an artist, a filmmaker, and Editor-in-Chief of *Quill and Parchment*. She has published three books of poetry and co-authored a book on film-production design.

Elda Lepak resides in Hendersonville, North Carolina. She is retired, yet her mind and body keep active through travel, grandchildren, kayaking, hiking, golfing, reading, and researching her family roots. All provide subjects for her poetry and photography.

Amelia Levchenko is a freshman in the Honors Program at the University of Wyoming, majoring in Dance and Theatre. "Oyster Girl" is from her collection of poems, *Buffalo Dancers in the Heart of America*, which chronicles her high school experiences.

Ellaraine Lockie is a poet, a nonfiction writer, an essayist, and a hand papermaker who has received eleven Pushcart nominations and many awards. Her most recent publication is an art broadside, *Mod Gods and Luggage Straps,* from *BrickBat Revue*.

Elizabeth Mastin lives in Coeur d'Alene, Idaho, where she is the lunch coordinator for Habitat for Humanity. She is indebted to her poetry mentor, Peter Lawlor, Poet Laureate of Whidbey Island, whose home is the sea.

Jeri McCormick is from Madison, Wisconsin. She was awarded a Wisconsin Arts Board Fellowship and has received several awards in Ireland. Her book, *When It Came Time*, was published by Ireland's Salmon Publishing, Ltd., and won an Outstanding Achievement Award from the Wisconsin Library Association.

Stephen Mead is an artist and writer living in northeastern New York. His poetry has appeared in *Bellowing Ark, Onionhead,* and *Invert.* His artwork is an eclectic blend of cubism, classic, and modern imagery.

Don Melcher is a retired engineer from Chicago, now living in rural Wisconsin. He has studied painting at the American Academy of Art. Melcher does volunteer work for the local Interfaith and Hospice, which includes working with some homeless persons.

Roger Midgett has won poetry awards from *Return to Creativity* and *The Presence Journal*. As a mental health professional in Seattle, he often works with people who are homeless.

Denise Amodeo Miller is a poet, writer, and teacher living in Buffalo, New York. She is an active member of The Buffalo Writers Meetup. Her award-winning poetry appeared in *Sol Magazine* Spring 2006, and others in two local anthologies.

P. C. Moorehead finds meaning in solitude, silence, and the beauty of nature. These nurture her relationships with others. A retired therapist, she appreciates having time to express herself creatively.

Wilda Morris is the author of a nonfiction book, *Stop the Violence! Educating Ourselves to Protect Our Youth*, and of *Szechwan Shrimp and Fortune Cookies: Poems from a Chinese Restaurant*.

Joshua Moses is a Ph.D. candidate in Anthropology at the Graduate Center of the City University of New York. He is a Ruth L. Kirchstein Fellow with the National Institute of Mental Health and Research Director for the New York City Zen Center for Contemplative Care.

Bruce Muench is a Navy veteran of W.W.II. Professionally, he is an aquatic biologist, having worked throughout the United States for the past sixty years. He sometimes serves at a soup kitchen in Rockford, Illinois.

Pamela Olson works as an advocate for children with disabilities in Alabama. She has been writing poetry for a number of years. She is married with two adult children.

Helen Padway lives, works, and laughs in Glendale, Wisconsin. She thinks poets tell the truth and can motivate us to make the world a better place.

Kathleen H. Phillips' life experiences as daughter, sister, wife, mother, grandmother, observant walker, and curious traveler have found their way into her poetry. She is grateful to Wisconsin's many creative poets for their inspiration and support; they have made the past nine years of writing a joy for her. She lives in Waukesha, Wisconsin.

David S. Pointer currently resides in Murfreesboro, Tennessee, with his two daughters. He has published widely in small presses and recently had a young-reader poem on display at the Mauch Chunk Museum in Jim Thorpe, Pennsylvania.

John J. Quirk is a member of Chicago's Homeless Action Committee and a representative on the All-Agency Member's Council of Thresholds, a social-service organization for persons who are both homeless and psychologically disabled.

Gamze Randolph is originally from Istanbul, Turkey. She feels blessed by the love and care she receives from her Turkish and American families. She hopes that every person in need of a warm home and love will one day find it.

Patrick T. Randolph and his soul-inspiring wife, Gamze, live on the banks of the mighty Mississippi River. He teaches academic and creative writing in the English as a Second Language Department at the University of Wisconsin-La Crosse. The homeless have been a central part of his psyche since 1990.

Gerald R. Randolph and his wife, Darlene, live in Rice Lake, Wisconsin. He is a retired English professor who fills his afternoons with woodworking, writing *tanka*, and winking at his wife. Randolph moved his family from the city to the woods in 1970, where he ran a self-sufficient farm in northwestern Wisconsin.

Liz Rhodebeck is a volunteer at the Food Pantry of Waukesha County. She has published poetry in *Margie* and *Free Verse* and helps organize the annual Food for the Heart and the Hungry Poetry Reading to benefit the pantry.

Jenna Rindo worked as a nursing assistant on a neuro floor and then as a pediatric intensive care nurse. She now teaches English as a Second Language to Hmong, Arabic, and Spanish students. She believes one kind action leads to another.

Lou Roach, a former psychotherapist, writes poetry and freelance articles in Poynette, Wisconsin. She has written two collections of poems: *A Different Muse* and *For Now*.

Ruth Sabath Rosenthal is a New York poet who treasures the fact that she has a good roof over her head, under which she writes poetry that has been published in such literary journals as *Connecticut Review* and *Jabberwock*. In October 2006, Rosenthal was nominated for a Pushcart Prize.

Judy Roy is a retired psychologist and French teacher. She writes poetry in the boreal forest of Door County. Her work has been published in *Wisconsin People & Ideas*, *Free Verse*, *The Peninsula Pulse*, *Hummingbird*, and other publications. She is a co-author of the chapbook *Slightly Off Q*.

Clara Sala is a poet, a singer, and an educator. Her work is informed by the unity of flesh, heart, and spirit. She often writes for those whose voices are seldom heard: women, children, the homeless, and the poor.

Nancy Scott is a social worker, an activist, and a foster and adoptive parent. She has spent decades helping homeless families and children find housing. Scott has turned many of her experiences into poetry.

Shizue Seigel's grandparents managed a single-room occupancy hotel in Stockton, California. Their children were too poor to realize they were poor; their wealth was in their hearts.

Noel Sloboda lives in Pennsylvania, with his wife and several rescued cats and dogs. He is the author of the poetry collection *Shell Games*.

Lester Smith is president of the Wisconsin Fellowship of Poets and the primary motivator behind Popcorn Press. Days he works as a writer and technologist for an educational publishing house. He lives in Delavan, Wisconsin, with his wife and best friend, Jenny.

Henrietta Sparks lives in Carpinteria, California, a small town near Santa Barbara. She retired from counseling at a Community College and a private therapy practice. Her poetry comes from these experiences and is always about relationships. Sparks spends her time writing, reading poetry, walking on the beach, and mucking around in tide pools.

Spiel spends about sixty hours per week making paintings or writing poetry about personal conflict and social consciousness. He has been involved in the arts all seven decades of his life.

J. J. Steinfeld has published a novel; nine short story collections, the most recent being *Would You Hide Me?* (Gaspereau Press); and a poetry collection, *An Affection for Precipices* (Serengeti Press). He resides on Prince Edward Island, Canada.

Mary Jo Stich, native of Illinois, now of New Denmark, Wisconsin, uses her hilltop home as inspiration for poetry, photography, and music. Gardening is thrown in for good measure.

Dorothy Stone's core was shaped in North Dakota; New York theatre added sparkle; and New England provided the home where she and her late husband shared their love affair with words.

Julian I. Taber worked in the Veterans Administration, treating veterans made homeless as a result of pathological gambling, alcoholism, and other addictions. His most recent book is titled *Addictions Anonymous*.

Katrin Talbot's poetry collection, *St. Cecilia's Daze*, is to be published by Parallel Press. Her mother's work for an Australian aid agency has given her a lifetime awareness of hunger and poverty. Talbot also seeks poetry while working with subtle images in her photography.

Susan F. Kirch-Thibado currently lives in Menomonie, Wisconsin, with her husband, Wayne. Kirch-Thibado has taught poetry classes to adults through the organization *Individual Learning in Retirement* and has had her work published in several state and national publications. Along with writing, gardening and yoga keep her soul balanced.

June Thompson does freelance writing for the *Marshfield News-Herald*. She lives in Neillsville, Wisconsin. Thompson has had poems published in *Free Verse* and *The Rockford Review*. She tries to focus her writings on the human condition. Thompson is currently writing a memoir.

Mary Langer Thompson's writing appears in various journals. Currently an educator in

California, she wants people to know that homeless children attend public schools, and that is where we can begin to help.

Larry Wahler "came of age" with a rucksack on his back, crisscrossing most of America while learning the spirit of homelessness in soup kitchens by day and under cold bridges at night.

Cecilia Woloch is the author of four award-winning collections of poems. Currently a lecturer at the University of Southern California, she has also conducted workshops in schools, prisons, community centers, and a shelter for homeless women.

Bill Zavatsky published *Where X Marks the Spot* in 2006. *The Poems of A. O. Barnabooth* by Valery Larbaud, co-translated with Ron Padgett, was reissued in 2008. He lives in New York City and teaches English at the Trinity School.

About the Editor and His Wife

Gamze and Patrick T. Randolph live near the banks of the mighty Mississippi River. Patrick grew up on a lake in the white birch, soft green pinewoods of northwestern Wisconsin. He has had an eclectic history of occupations, including two different experiences in which he worked for the homeless in Chicago and San Francisco. For the past 14 years, he has been teaching English as a Second Language—both in the States and abroad. Currently, he teaches at the University of Wisconsin-La Crosse. Gamze is originally from Istanbul, Turkey, the mystical city which fuses a kaleidoscope of humanity brimming with endless poetry. Her interests include crafts, film, art, traveling, and caring for her Turkish and American families. She is currently an MBA student at the same university where Patrick teaches. Gamze and Patrick dance the dance of life, laughter, and help those in need of a hug.

About
Popcorn Press

Popcorn Press is a micropublishing house based in southern Wisconsin, devoted to publishing fiction and poetry that is both genuine and unique.

Visit us on the Web at www.PopcornPress.com.